W9-BAL-217

How Renewable Energy Is Changing Society

Robert Green

Science, Technology, and Society

ReferencePoint Press®

San Diego, CA

About the Author

Robert Green writes about the politics of Hong Kong and Taiwan for the Economist Intelligence Unit and for Oxford Analytica and regularly reviews books on topics related to East Asia. He holds master's degrees from New York University and Harvard. He first became interested in science writing by exploring the imaginative tales of Jules Verne.

© 2016 ReferencePoint Press, Inc.
Printed in the United States

For more information, contact:
ReferencePoint Press, Inc.
PO Box 27779
San Diego, CA 92198
www.ReferencePointPress.com

Picture Credits:
Cover: Thinkstock Images; Maury Aaseng, 16, 43, 57; Associated Press, 34; © Thomas Barrat/Shutterstock, 7 (top); © Bettmann/Corbis, 21; © Gary Braasch/Corbis, 47; Deposit Photos, 7 (bottom), 10, 14, 39, 69; Kevin Dietsch/UPI/Newscom, 66; © Everett Historical/Shutterstock, 6 (bottom left); © FB-Rose/imageBROKER/Corbis, 64; © Imaginechina/Corbis, 52; © Neijia/Shutterstock, 6 (bottom right); © Jose Fuste Raga/Corbis, 59; © Shawn Thew/epa/Corbis, 31; © Triff/Shutterstock, 6 (top); © Tony Waltham/Robert Harding World Imagery/Corbis, 27

LIBRARY OF CONGRESS CATALOGING-IN-PUBLICATION DATA

Green, Robert, 1969-
  How renewable energy is changing society / by Robert Green.
    pages cm. -- (Science, technology, and society)
  Audience: Grade 9 to 12.
  Includes bibliographical references and index.
  ISBN-13: 978-1-60152-904-6 (hardback)
  ISBN-10: 1-60152-904-X (hardback) 1. Renewable energy sources--Social aspects--Juvenile literature. 2. Renewable energy sources--Juvenile literature. 3. Energy policy--Juvenile literature. I. Title.
  TJ808.G675 2016
  303.48'3--dc23
                                                                    2015009487

Contents

"Science and technology have had a major impact on society, and their impact is growing. By drastically changing our means of communication, the way we work, our housing, clothes, and food, our methods of transportation, and, indeed, even the length and quality of life itself, science has generated changes in the moral values and basic philosophies of mankind.

"Beginning with the plow, science has changed how we live and what we believe. By making life easier, science has given man the chance to pursue societal concerns such as ethics, aesthetics, education, and justice; to create cultures; and to improve human conditions. But it has also placed us in the unique position of being able to destroy ourselves."

— Donald P. Hearth, former director of the NASA Langley Research Center, 1985.

Donald P. Hearth wrote these words in 1985. They appear in the foreword of a publication titled *The Impact of Science on Society*, a collection of speeches given during a public lecture series of the same name. Although Hearth's words were written about three decades ago, they are as true today as when they first appeared on the page.

Advances in science and technology undeniably bring about societal change. Gene therapy, for instance, has the potential to revolutionize medicine and the treatment of debilitating illnesses such as sickle-cell anemia and Parkinson's disease. Medical experts say gene therapy might also be used to treat conditions ranging from obesity to depression and someday, perhaps, even to help extend human life spans.

Although gene therapy offers great hope and promise, it also carries significant risks. The 1999 death of an eighteen-year-old patient taking part in a gene therapy clinical trial in the United States provided a painful reminder of the need for strict safeguards and monitoring. Other risks may be less tangible for the time being, but they are no less serious. The idea of changing the genetic instructions for human beings can be construed in some instances as arrogant, immoral, and dangerous. The possibility of making such changes raises questions of who should decide which traits are normal and desirable and which are to be considered unhealthy. It raises questions about the enhancement of the intellectual and athletic capabilities of individuals and about the potential for discrimination against those judged to be in possession of less desirable or faulty genes.

ReferencePoint's *Science, Technology, and Society* series examines scientific and technological advances in the context of their impact on society. Topics covered in the series include gene therapy, the Internet, renewable energy, robotics, and mobile devices. Each book explores how and why this science or technology came about; how it has influenced or shaped daily life and culture; efforts to guide or control the technology through laws and policies; and what the next generation of this technology might look like. Included in the chapters are focus questions aimed at eliciting conversation and debate. Also included are key words and terms and their meanings in the context of the topics covered. Fully documented quotes enliven the narrative and add to the usefulness of the series as a tool for student researchers.

The study of science, technology, and society—sometimes referred to as STS—has gained significant ground in recent years. Top universities, including Stanford and UC Berkeley in California and MIT and Harvard in Massachusetts, are among the many that offer majors or specialized programs devoted to the study of science, technology, and society. The National Science Foundation, an independent federal agency created by Congress in 1950, even has a program that funds research and education specifically on this topic. For secondary students interested in this field, or for those who are merely curious or just trying to fulfill an assignment, ReferencePoint's new series can provide a useful and accessible starting point.

1839
French physicist Edmond Becquerel discovers the photovoltaic effect, by which solar energy is converted into electricity.

1869
French scientist Augustin Mouchot publishes *Solar Heat and Its Industrial Applications* and unveils a solar-powered steam engine that produces electricity.

1908
Henry Ford designs his original Model T to run not on gasoline, a fossil fuel, but on ethanol, a biofuel that has since come back into fashion as an alternative to gasoline.

1966
France constructs a large-scale electricity station derived from the movement of the tides near the estuary of the Rance River.

1882
US inventor Thomas Edison builds the first electric power plant, located in lower New York City.

1921
Albert Einstein wins the Nobel Prize in Physics for his study of the photovoltaic effect; through his work he is able to explain how energy is derived from sunlight.

1958
The National Aeronautics and Space Administration launches *Vanguard I* into space; it carries photovoltaic cells that power its radios.

1970
US president Richard Nixon establishes the US Environmental Protection Agency due to growing concerns about pollution and other environmental issues.

2011
A meltdown at Japan's Fukushima Daiichi Nuclear Power Plant, which was hit by an earthquake-triggered tsunami, spurs antinuclear sentiment around the globe.

1979
US president Jimmy Carter installs solar panels on the roof of the White House to raise awareness for alternative energy during an oil embargo by Middle Eastern oil producers.

2008
China completes the Three Gorges Dam, the world's largest hydroelectric power plant.

1978
The US Congress requires public utilities to buy a certain amount of electricity from renewable energy sources.

2009
At the United Nations Climate Change Conference, scientists argue that global temperature increases should be kept below 3.6°F (2°C).

2013
The price of solar energy per megawatt reaches parity with coal in some parts of the United States and in other countries, including India and Italy.

2014
Germany for the first time produces more energy from renewable sources than from any other energy source, accounting for 27 percent of its energy supplies.

Alternating Currents

When Thomas Edison, one of America's most celebrated inventors, flipped on the electricity in New York City's first electric power station on September 4, 1882, he set America on a new course. As the electricity pumped through the copper coils, the soft glow of his lightbulbs illuminated a square mile at the heart of America's financial capital.

The *New York Times*, which saw its offices lit for the first time by electric light, recorded the sensation in the following day's newspaper. "Then the 27 electric lamps in the editorial rooms and the 25 lamps in the counting rooms made those departments as bright as day," marveled the newspaper. "It was a light that a man could sit down under and write for hours without the consciousness of having any artificial light about him."[1]

No longer would Americans need to work by the flicker of candlelight or gas lamp. The switch to electrification had begun. Soon electric elevators allowed builders to erect towering skyscrapers, illuminated by electric light and cooled in the summer by electric air-conditioning. Access to central supplies of electricity transformed America's cities and reshaped society. Electricity led to the invention of refrigerators, televisions, and a myriad of other gizmos and appliances that shaped the patterns of modern life.

As energy demands rose, scientists raced for even cheaper methods to produce it. The frontiers of energy production seemed full of promise. By the 1950s energy harvested from the atom, known as nuclear energy, offered the possibility of undreamed-of supplies of cheap energy. In 1954 the head of the US Atomic Energy Commission believed that "the next generation will have electricity so cheap it won't be metered."[2]

That sunny optimism became a hallmark of America's can-do, fast-paced society. But the breakneck economic growth was built largely on the consumption of ever-greater supplies of energy. And that energy, it turned out, was threatening to forever change the earth's climate.

Dire Predictions

Edison's 1882 electric power station, like so many that came after it, was fueled by coal. In 2013, 39 percent of all US electricity still relied on the burning of coal—the dirtiest of all the fossil fuels. Fossil fuels—coal, oil, and natural gas—have been the primary source of energy fueling modern industry.

When burned, however, fossil fuels release gases that heat the earth's atmosphere. The gases act like panes of glass in a greenhouse by trapping the heat of the sun's rays inside the atmosphere. The gases, therefore, are known as greenhouse gases, and scientists believe that these human-made emissions are causing atmospheric temperatures to rise. This process is generally known as global warming, though others refer to it as climate change to highlight the breadth of climatic changes that could result from rising temperatures.

Fossil fuels today account for about 80 percent of the world's energy supply, and their use has grown rapidly as economies around the globe have industrialized. "If 'business as usual' continues," argue scientists Richard K. Lester and David M. Hart, "before the end of the century the world is likely to experience climate change on a devastating scale."[3]

> **greenhouse gases**
>
> Gases such as carbon dioxide and methane that absorb the sun's infrared radiation, trapping it in the form of heat in the earth's atmosphere.

Renewable Optimism

Gloomy predictions like this have sparked a global debate on how humans should produce and consume energy. The currents of the debate run through society in many ways. Governments hash out

The Manhattan skyline lights up New York City at night. A centralized and steady supply of electricity transformed the look and character of US cities and reshaped modern society.

energy policy at international conferences, while individuals make daily decisions about their own energy use. Today people sometimes speak of their carbon footprint, a measure of how much an individual contributes to the greenhouse gases that cause global warming. Awareness of the potential environmental consequences of burning fossil fuels has entered into the consciousness of everyday people.

That awareness has in turn spurred calls for new approaches to energy production and a search for alternatives to fossil fuels. The ultimate prize in this energy quest is the development of nonfossil-fuel energy sources, which cannot be depleted and do not release greenhouse gases. These alternative energy sources are known as renewable sources of energy, since unlike fossil fuels, they cannot be depleted. Renewable energy is derived from natural phenomena such as the movement of rivers (hydroelectric), the heat of the sun (solar), the heat from the earth's interior (geothermal), and the currents of the wind. Tapping their potential could transform society.

carbon footprint

A measure of the greenhouse gases produced by human activity; it can refer to either an individual or a group of people.

"If a transition to renewable is really made on a large scale," writes Pulitzer Prize–winning author Daniel Yergin, "it will rival the importance of the world's transition to reliance on oil in the twentieth century."[4]

That search for a new long-term solution for the world's energy needs seems to be running on a strange mix of conflicting emotional currents. On the one hand, fear of rising seas, sinking coastlines, and catastrophic storms has driven support for renewable energy. On the other hand, the possibility of abandoning fossil fuels drives optimism over the potential of renewable energy. Today's energy entrepreneurs and scientists are just as optimistic as Edison was in 1882. And the stakes are just as great. Their success or failure will largely shape the kind of global society humans inhabit in the near and distant future.

The Rise of Renewable Energy

"I'd put my money on the sun and solar energy. What a source of power!"

—Thomas Edison, inventor.

Quoted in Heather Rodgers, "Current Thinking," *New York Times*, June 3, 2007. www.nytimes.com.

Thomas Edison, who did so much to introduce Americans to electric lighting, realized early on the shortcomings of coal. It had to be dug out of the ground, shipped to furnaces in cities, and burned nonstop to produce the electricity that fired his light-giving bulbs. There were two main problems with coal in Edison's day, and they are problems that still trouble societies that rely on coal-generated power today. First, coal is finite—there is only so much of it buried beneath the earth. Second, burning coal to fuel electric power plants releases pollutants into the atmosphere.

Coal shares these drawbacks with the other common fossil fuels—oil and natural gas. They are called fossil fuels because they are created from the fossilized remains of ancient plant and animal matter long buried beneath the earth's surface. The energy that can be extracted from fossil fuels is actually the sun's energy trapped by the once-living matter and transformed over time into dense carbon deposits—in the form of goopy oil, stonelike coal, or invisible natural gas. Fossil fuels, for this reason, are also known as carbon-based fuels.

The burning of fossil fuels provides most of the energy used today. But this was not always the case. In the remote past, humans relied both on fossil fuels and nonfossil fuels. The burning of fossil fuels proved useful for the creation of light (burning oil in lamps) and heat (burning coal for the shaping of metals), but other sources of energy were even more commonly used.

Simple innovations allowed ancient humans to make use of naturally occurring renewable energy sources, most notably the sun and the wind. Ancient Egyptians, for example, situated their homes to soak up the sun's heat during the day and release it during the cooler hours of the night. They also captured the wind's energy in cloth sails that propelled their ships along the Nile River.

Putting the Wind to Work

Even in antiquity, renewable energy sources powered machinery. In Persia (present-day Iran), the rotating arms of simple windmills moved a shaft that could be used to crush grain. It was so beneficial to allow the wind to help with this daily chore that other societies also adopted windmills. But it was not until the industrial age that the energy potential of wind was put to work for a different purpose—the creation of electricity.

In Edison's day inventors attempted to create electricity by harnessing the wind as an alternative to burning coal. There was no particular reason that this could not be done, at least in theory. Coal actually serves a very limited function in an electric power plant. It is burned solely to create heat. The heat then boils water, which gives off steam. The steam is pressurized as it flows through pipes, and the pressurized steam turns a turbine, a mechanical spinning device that creates electricity.

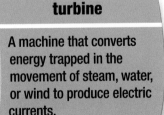

turbine

A machine that converts energy trapped in the movement of steam, water, or wind to produce electric currents.

The key to the generation of electricity is in fact not the heat but the spinning motion of the turbine. Early inventors realized that electricity could therefore be generated by using other sources of motion, such as the wind, to turn the turbine.

In separate experiments in 1887, a pair of professors attempted to use the wind's energy to power Edison's electric lightbulb. One was a Scottish electrical engineer named James Blyth; the

Coal is a cheap and reliable power source, but it has two major shortcomings: It is a finite resource and the burning of coal for power releases pollutants into the atmosphere.

other was American inventor Charles Brush, who had been experimenting with electricity since age twelve. Both men, driven by the desire to light their homes with renewable energy, constructed windmills as a power source.

Once completed, the windmills looked quite different. Blyth's was smaller and spun parallel to the ground. Brush, on the other hand, assembled a giant wheel spinning perpendicularly to the ground, much the way windmills do today. But both achieved the same revolutionary result—they generated electricity solely by using the wind's energy to power a turbine.

The wind turbines required no burning, and they created no pollution. Yet there was the electricity, humming through copper wires and illuminating bulbs throughout both men's houses. The two inventors proved that renewable energy had the potential to replace coal in the production of electricity—if it could be harnessed on a large scale. According to the eminent Scottish physicist William Thompson, it was not "utterly chimerical to think of wind superseding coal in some places for a very important part of its present duty—that of giving light."[5]

Electrifying the Sun's Rays

Like wind energy, solar energy has an ancient pedigree. The sun has been used for centuries to warm homes and heat water supplies and later to cook food by concentrating the sun's energy to act as a heat source. In the nineteenth century, even before Blyth and Brush converted wind energy into electricity, scientists were tinkering with machines that could generate electricity from sunlight.

The nineteenth century was an electricity-obsessed age, and the science behind converting sunlight into electricity progressed in a series of slow, and often disconnected, steps by different scientists. One of the earliest breakthroughs occurred in 1839 when French scientist Edmond Becquerel created a simple solar cell by inserting two metal plates (intended to conduct the electricity) into an acidic solution that formed a circuit through which electricity could run. When Becquerel exposed this circuit to sunlight, he observed that an electric current was created. Becquerel's simple solar conductor was, in fact, converting sunlight into electricity. It was a remarkable discovery, made even more remarkable by the fact that he was only nineteen years old at the time.

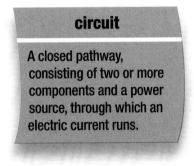

circuit

A closed pathway, consisting of two or more components and a power source, through which an electric current runs.

What Becquerel had observed is a phenomenon known as the photovoltaic effect. The first part of this term, *photo*, is derived from the ancient Greek word for "light." The second part, *voltaic*, means "having to do with electricity." *Voltaic* is in fact derived from the name of Italian scientist Alessandro Volta, who invented the electric battery—the energy of which is measured in volts.

Despite Becquerel's breakthrough in unlocking the potential to turn sunlight directly into electricity, practical application would take years to master. In fact, it was not until 1905 that Albert Einstein, the world's most celebrated physicist, explained the phenomenon

The Modern Photovoltaic Cell

Edmond Becquerel's simple solar cell represented a breakthrough in efforts to convert sunlight into electricity. Years later, physicist Albert Einstein explained the science behind the solar cell, a phenomenon known as the photovoltaic effect. Many more years passed before the development of the modern solar, or photovoltaic, cell. As the National Aeronautics and Space Administration (NASA) explains on its website: In the basic photovoltaic cell, "a thin semiconductor wafer is specially treated to form an electric field, positive on one side and negative on the other. When light energy strikes the solar cell, electrons are knocked loose from the atoms in the semiconductor material. If electrical conductors are attached to the positive and negative sides, forming an electrical circuit, the electrons can be captured in the form of an electric current—that is, electricity. This electricity can then be used to power a load, such as a light or a tool."

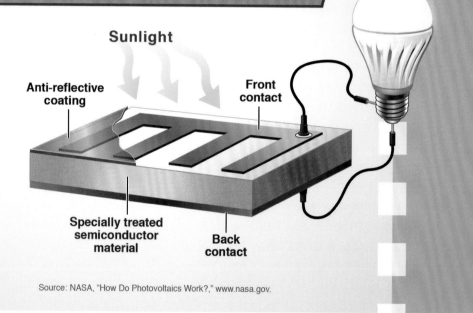

Sunlight

Anti-reflective coating

Front contact

Specially treated semiconductor material

Back contact

Source: NASA, "How Do Photovoltaics Work?," www.nasa.gov.

through mathematics, a feat for which he later won a Nobel Prize. Even with Einstein's description of photons, or packets of light, scientists struggled to find a workable model for the technology that had been proved first in practice by Becquerel and then in theory by Einstein.

In fact, it was not until 1954, building on another half century of experiments, that scientists working at Bell Laboratories demonstrated a prototype for a commercial solar cell at their headquarters in Murray Hill, New Jersey. The scientists of Bell Laboratories put their solar cell to work turning a Ferris wheel to demonstrate the potential of solar energy to power machinery. The demonstration impressed the *New York Times*, which wrote that solar energy "may mark the beginning of a new era, leading eventually to the realization of one of mankind's most cherished dreams—the harnessing of the almost limitless energy of the sun for the uses of civilization."[6]

> **photovoltaic effect**
>
> The process by which an electric current is produced by exposing certain substances to sunlight.

Gizmos for the Science Minded

The excited commentary from the *New York Times* was typical of the widespread optimism for the potential uses of renewable energy from both the sun and the wind. Companies like Bell Laboratories raced to find commercial applications and make profits. The development of both of these sources of energy, however, languished. The problem was a simple one, but with no easy solution. The new technologies could create electricity, but only at much higher costs than coal. As a result, they were seen as hobbies for scientists and dreamers—a future technology whose day had not yet arrived.

Despite solar energy's potential, applications remained limited to organizations with astronomical budgets. The best customer in the 1950s, in fact, was the US military, which ran the US space program before it was transferred to the National Aeronautics and Space Administration (NASA), which was created in 1958. Because fuel cells had to be as small as possible to fit on spacecraft and because the US government had a large budget, early solar technology was eagerly adopted for the space program.

In 1958, for example, the US Navy launched *Vanguard I*, a 3-pound (1.4 kg) mini-satellite only 6 inches (15 cm) in diameter. The United States was at the time engaged in a space race with the Soviet Union, and when Soviet leader Nikita Khrushchev heard of the tiny size, he mocked it as a "grapefruit satellite."[7]

Vanguard I, however, had a feature that made it a rather remarkable mini-satellite. After transmitting information back to Earth for twenty days, its conventional batteries died. But the solar panels fixed on the tiny orb then took over. Using only solar energy, *Vanguard I* continued to transmit readings from space for another seven years—reliant only on the sun's rays streaming through space as its sole source of power. Since then, solar panels have regularly been used in space, where conventional energy supplies cannot be easily replenished.

The space program succeeded in putting solar energy to practical use, but society was still trying to find affordable ways to use the sun's energy in daily life. Ultimately, solar energy powered some rather surprising innovations. In 1968 miniature solar panels were fixed to wristwatches, and for the first time the sun powered something that regular people used in daily life. But the craze for solar gizmos really kicked in a decade later when companies mass-produced inexpensive solar calculators, though they tended not to work well indoors, where they were most often used.

Despite the limited use of these early solar-powered devices, solar energy had fired the imagination of the public. But solar energy was still contributing very little to the world's rapidly growing electricity demands. The easiest renewable source of energy to harness, it turned out, was neither the sun nor the wind, but the swift-moving rivers being pulled by gravity toward the sea.

Harnessing the Rivers

Ancient energy prospectors, searching for naturally occurring sources of power, could sometimes rely on their ears for clues to hidden sources of energy. The sound of winds howling over prairies reflected pent-up energy potential that could be captured by windmills. The thunderous crashing of cataracts and the steady rumble of swift-moving rivers indicated that energy could also be harnessed from the world's river systems.

The ancient Greeks used waterwheels to capture the energy of moving water in much the same way as windmills captured the energy of moving air. The Greeks designed a simple wooden wheel with paddles, fixed it on a pole, and dipped the paddles

The Sun's Rays in War and Peace

Using mirrors to concentrate the energy of the sun turned out to be a surprisingly common pursuit for the scientists of ancient Greece. In a study titled *On Burning Mirrors*, the Greek mathematician Diocles noted how curved reflectors focused the heat energy of the sun. Archimedes, a fellow mathematician with a gift for invention, put the theory into action when the Romans besieged his native Syracuse, a Greek city-state on the Italian island of Sicily. According to legend, he used polished metal, possibly from the shields of the Greek warriors, to focus sunlight into burning rays that ignited the sails of the Roman ships.

Directing the sun's rays in this manner is similar to burning leaves with a magnifying glass. With the magnifying glass, however, it is the curvature of the lens that concentrates the sunlight as it passes through the glass. Concentrating sunlight to produce heat creates what is known as solar thermal energy.

In the quest to build better solar panels, innovators have reproduced Archimedes' method of intensifying sunlight, but for peaceful purposes. Generally, these solar installations feature long, curved reflectors through which a suspended pipe runs. The curved reflectors concentrate the sun's energy on the pipe and heat the fluid inside. This fluid then carries the heat to a turbine that converts it into electricity.

into the river. Rushing river water propelled the paddles in an endless rhythm. The wheel, in turn, spun a shaft to which grain-milling machinery was attached. The water mills thus allowed humans to save their own energy for other essential tasks while the water crushed grain for human consumption.

During the nineteenth-century scramble for new sources of electricity, scientists realized that turbines could be powered in the same way as the ancient waterwheels. In 1881 a turbine was attached to a water mill located near the powerful cascades at Niagara Falls, situated on the US-Canadian border. The electricity it generated illuminated streetlights in the town of Niagara Falls, New York.

Converting the energy of swift-moving river waters into electricity was an attractive idea on its own. But hydroelectric power was even more appealing because it could solve two problems at once. Dams could be constructed that both generated electricity and controlled the unpredictable flow of rivers. Before turbines were attached to dams, the sole purpose of dams was to control the volume of water flowing through a river.

A dam shifted control over the river's waters from nature to humans. Reservoirs above a dam could be released when the river's waters were low and replenished when the winter snows melted or heavy rains fell. Thus, the damming of rivers helped ensure stable farming and prevented the flooding of communities situated near major river systems. Eventually, the production of electricity was added to the dam's duties.

Renewable Energy at Work

During the worldwide economic slowdown of the 1930s, known as the Great Depression, the US government struggled to address falling crop production, unemployment, and general panic. States surrounding portions of the Tennessee River were particularly hard hit by the Depression. To stimulate economic activity in the area, newly elected president Franklin Roosevelt created the Tennessee Valley Authority (TVA). The agency immediately put unemployed Americans to work constructing a series of dams on the Tennessee River. The project thus created both jobs and cheap electricity to stimulate other economic activity in the region.

So successful was the TVA that the experiment was replicated in other parts of the country. In Washington State, for example, an army of workers began to dam the Columbia River in 1933. The river system already had smaller dams intended to regulate the floodwaters, but the Grand Coulee Dam would prove to be a marvel of power generation.

The dam's walls, rising some 550 feet (168 m) from their foundation in the granite riverbed below, funneled the river's swift-moving waters through eighteen generators located within two power plants, situated on the left and right sides of the dam. Two more generators were later added to pump out even more electricity. The dam turned the once untamable river into a powerhouse for the region's industrial activity.

The Grand Coulee Dam in Washington is a marvel of power generation. The dam turned the seemingly untamable Columbia River into a powerhouse for industrial activity.

Roosevelt, who campaigned for the presidency on expanding hydroelectric power in 1932, believed that harnessing the power of America's rivers could restart the economy and help lift the United States out of economic depression. "This vast water power can be of incalculable value to this whole section of the country,"[8] he said in Portland, Oregon, in 1933. Indeed, the Grand Coulee's energy output lived up to this ambitious goal. Today it provides more than 70 percent of Washington State's electricity and exports electricity to ten other states and Canada.

Roosevelt's drive for hydroelectric power rapidly increased US energy supplies without adding to the air pollution created by the burning of fossil fuels. By 1940 hydroelectric power supplied 40 percent of all US electricity. Since then, hydroelectricity generated by America's dams has remained relatively steady, but energy demands have continued to rise. In 2013 hydroelectric power

China's Mega Dam

When Washington State's Grand Coulee Dam was completed in 1942, it was the largest single source of electric power in the United States, and it remains so today. Its electric capacity, however, has since been dwarfed by a Chinese mega dam called the Three Gorges Dam, which harnesses the renewable energy of the Yangtze River.

The dam itself spans 1.5 miles (2.4 km) and has walls that rise some 600 feet (183 m) up from the bedrock. Its thirty-two electricity-producing turbines at peak performance can generate 22,500 megawatts of electricity, more than three times as much as the Grand Coulee Dam and just under three times as much electricity as the world's largest nuclear power plant. Perhaps the most unusual feature of the massive dam complex is a system of locks that allows oceangoing freighters to navigate the Yangtze—connecting the coast with the interior of the vast country.

Like non-electricity-producing dams, the Three Gorges Dam also regulates the flooding of the Yangtze, which historically has caused countless deaths and considerable disruption to villages along the river system. The massive reservoir created by the dam, however, has resulted in human-made flooding, frequent erosion of the banks of the river and the reservoir, and an increase in earth-quakes in the region. Environmentalists lament the destruction of the river's eco-system, and government sources estimate that over 1 million people have been forced out of their homes to accommodate this colossal project.

accounted for only 7 percent of US electricity supplies, far outstripped by the amount of electricity created by burning coal.

Damming more rivers, moreover, often draws public opposition. Dams change the local ecosystem, impacting fish in the river itself and wildlife surrounding the river. They can also displace people and flood private property. Even without new dams, the electricity-generating capacity of rivers is still increasing. This is because old dams are being upgraded with new generations of turbines that create more electricity, and old dams can be retrofitted with turbines to further add capacity.

According to the US Department of Energy, hydroelectric power can be augmented by 15 percent of its current capacity by these methods alone. "One of the best opportunities we have to increase our supply of clean energy is by bringing our hydropower systems into the 21st Century," said Steven Chu, the US secretary of energy, in 2009. "With this investment, we can create jobs, help our environment and give more renewable power to our economy without building a single new dam."[9]

New Considerations

Despite the success of hydroelectric power in the United States, demand for ever more energy dwarfed the output of all renewable sources of energy. The mighty American industrial economy increasingly came to rely on fossil fuels in the decades after World War II. America's plentiful coal deposits provided much of the electricity supply, while America's cars ran on another fossil fuel that was imported from abroad in ever-greater quantities. This was of course oil, which can be refined into the gasoline that powers the engines of modern vehicles.

By the 1970s two factors made Americans take a fresh look at renewable energy sources as an alternative to cheap coal, oil, and natural gas. The first was the alarm caused by a sharp rise in pollution emitted from cars and power plants. Smoggy skies over American cities and dead fish in polluted rivers shocked Americans, who were growing concerned about fossil fuels' impact on the environment. But even as environmental concerns made people question the wisdom of burning fossil fuels, international political factors caused a more immediate crisis—one that dried up American supplies of gasoline when foreign governments cut off shipments to the United States. Both of these trends rekindled the search to find alternatives to fossil fuels.

The Search for Energy Independence

"No one can ever embargo the sun."

—Jimmy Carter, thirty-ninth president of the United States.

Jimmy Carter, "Solar Energy Remarks Announcing Administration Proposals," American Presidency Project, June 20, 1979. www.presidency.ucsb.edu.

The dangers of America's dependence on foreign oil first entered the popular imagination through images of cars lining up at gas stations running short on gasoline in 1973. The year was one of unrelenting bad news. The US president, Richard Nixon, had already imposed price controls on gasoline two years earlier, and that was causing the cost of almost everything to rise.

The United States was at the time the largest consumer of oil in the world. The American way of life, with its cheap gasoline and endless miles of highways, relied on cheap supplies of oil. Amid the economic frustration and long lines at the pump, the United States discovered that reliance on oil shipped from abroad presented a new type of national security problem. What if hostile nations cut off the oil supplies that America so desperately needed to fuel its economy?

That is just what happened in 1973 when a group of Middle Eastern oil producers halted all shipments to the United States. This oil embargo resulted from anger in some Middle Eastern countries over American support for Israel during the 1973 Arab-Israeli War. The Arab nations reasoned that since the United States supported their enemy during the conflict, they could punish the United States by halting oil shipments.

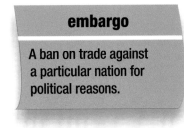

embargo

A ban on trade against a particular nation for political reasons.

"The Arabs had reached for the oil weapon, and their act would change the oil markets for decades, undermining stable price regimes," writes journalist Patrick Tyler. "The West was going to get hit hard."[10]

The United States was indeed hit hard. The oil embargo plunged the US economy into the worst recession since the Great Depression of the 1930s. Unemployment shot up, and the price of crude oil jumped from three dollars to nine dollars per barrel (cheap compared with today's prices but shocking at the time). Oil proved to be an extremely effective weapon, and it caused the giant American economy—the world's largest—to falter. "The crisis also dealt a blow to American prestige," write Gal Luft and Anne Korin in *Foreign Affairs*. "At the height of the Cold War, the United States essentially proved that without oil it was a paper tiger."[11]

America Struggles to Respond

The crisis resulting from the 1973 oil embargo is sometimes called the "oil shock." And it did indeed provide a jolt of energy through the US government, which scrambled to find a solution to this potentially crippling problem. Politicians from both the left and the right of the political spectrum—from the Democratic and Republican political parties—agreed that the United States must adopt a new energy policy to prevent other nations from using oil as a weapon.

On November, 25, 1973, Nixon delivered a nationally televised address identifying a priority that would be shared by every president who followed him into the White House—the quest for energy independence. "From its beginning 200 years ago, throughout its history, America has made great sacrifices of blood and also of treasure to achieve and maintain its independence," stated the somber-voiced Nixon. "In the last third of this century, our independence will depend on maintaining and achieving self-sufficiency in energy."[12]

In this address on energy, Nixon announced Project Independence, which would reduce America's reliance on Middle Eastern oil by two methods—conservation and increased drilling for domestic oil supplies. To cope with the immediate reduction of oil supplies caused by the embargo, Nixon advised Americans to tighten their belts. They could do this, he advised, by driving at slower speeds, turning down the heat, and keeping the lights off as much as possible.

These conservation methods were hardly welcome ideas to US consumers, who were used to burning ever-greater amounts of energy, driving when and where they wanted, and buying up electrical appliances to make life easier and more enjoyable.

The second part of the proposal was intended as a longer-term solution. Increased domestic drilling could tap newly discovered oil reserves in Alaska, thus increasing domestic oil supplies. Congress duly approved an Alaskan pipeline, which carried the oil across Alaska before it was shipped to the rest of the United States. Oil began coursing through the new pipeline in 1977. Few people at the time, however, believed that new domestic oil production would end the US reliance on foreign oil. The reason was that oil production in the United States was in fact rapidly declining.

Peak Oil

Whereas coal drove the Industrial Revolution in England, oil was to be closely associated with the rapid economic growth of the United States. It was in the United States that the world's first

Oil began coursing through the Trans-Alaska Pipeline (pictured) in 1977. The pipeline was conceived of as a means of reducing US reliance on Middle Eastern oil.

oil well was drilled, just outside Titusville, Pennsylvania, in 1859. Prospecting for oil, by adventurers known as wildcatters, initiated a new "gold rush" in which fortunes were wrenched from the earth not in the form of gold, but in oil gushing from newly discovered oil fields.

When wildcatters struck oil in the early days of prospecting, the oil often sprang out of wells with tremendous force. This was because the deposits were located near the surface, untapped and pressurized. "Lucky prospectors could just about pop a straw in the ground and release a gusher,"[13] writes journalist Amanda Little.

These oil fields could be exploited with ease, and the United States became the leading oil producer in the world. The oil fields, however, were exhaustible. When the oil near the earth's surface began to go dry, prospectors dug deeper and deeper in search of new oil supplies. Drilling in remote northern Alaska represented the tail end of this early stage of oil extraction. The easy stuff, in short, had already been pumped out and burned up. US oil production had already reached its peak in 1970, when wells produced a record high of 10 million barrels of oil per day.

This all-time-high point of production is referred to as peak oil. After the peak, production declines due to dwindling supplies. Although the United States once led the world in oil production, its oil supplies dropped sharply after 1970, as old oil wells dried up and prospectors found it increasingly difficult to find new oil.

A Day in the Sun

Even though US oil production began to decline after 1970, demand continued to rise. This meant that the United States imported ever-greater amounts of foreign oil. Nixon had promised to achieve energy independence by 1980, but this goal remained elusive. The fundamental flaw in his plan was the lack of an alternative source of energy. Aside from hydroelectric power, renewable energy was still in its infancy during Nixon's time in office. Conservation alone, the United States quickly discovered, would not significantly reduce the demand for oil.

An alternative to oil was embraced, however, by Jimmy Carter, who became president in 1977. Instead of conservation and domestic drilling, Carter wanted the United States to make use of advances in solar energy to help decrease oil imports. Importantly for his plan, the price for solar energy was dropping quickly. Measured in watts, the technology dropped from one hundred dollars to twenty dollars per watt in the 1970s alone. In the spring of 1977, Carter, like Nixon before him, addressed the nation on the subject of energy. He noted that domestic production of fossil fuels had been dropping by 6 percent a year. He therefore called for the rapid development of solar energy and set a goal of providing enough solar capacity to power 2.5 million homes by 1985.

In a public ceremony two years later, Carter unveiled solar panels that had been installed on the roof of the White House,

Three Mile Island

Advocates for energy independence had great hopes for producing domestic energy through nuclear technology. Tapping the power of the atom had the potential to provide an energy source that required no Middle Eastern imports. Advocates also noted that nuclear power plants released none of the polluting emissions of fossil-fuel-burning power plants.

Nuclear energy suffered a major blow, however, after an accident at Three Mile Island, a nuclear installation in Dauphin County, Pennsylvania. On March 28, 1979, the plant experienced a partial meltdown and released radioactive gases into the air. It was the worst nuclear accident in American history, and it triggered an antinuclear protest movement that continues to this day. The accident at Three Mile Island resulted in a slowdown in the construction of new nuclear facilities in the United States.

Subsequent nuclear accidents abroad, such as those in 1986 in Chernobyl, Ukraine, and in 2011 in Fukushima, Japan, have raised public concerns over the long-term safety of nuclear energy. Antinuclear sentiment has caused some nations, such as Sweden and Germany, to phase out nuclear technology altogether and others, such as Taiwan, to move in that direction. As a result, nuclear energy is unlikely to serve as a permanent replacement for fossil fuels.

the historic building that acts as both the home and the office of the president. "Today, in directly harnessing the power of the Sun, we're taking the energy that God gave us, the most renewable energy that we will ever see, and using it to replace our dwindling supplies of fossil fuels,"[14] he said.

In the Mix

To support his ambitious plan, Carter created the US Department of Energy, which coordinated energy policy and searched for alternative energy sources. The US Congress supported Carter's efforts at ensuring energy independence by passing the Energy Security Act, which Carter signed into law in 1980. During the ceremony, he called for solar energy to account for 20 percent of US energy needs by 2000.

Since the Carter presidency, renewable energy has been included in every subsequent president's energy plan, and the subject of energy has taken on an ever-greater importance in national life. "Every president since Nixon has placed energy security high on the list of presidential priorities,"[15] writes energy specialist Robert Rapier.

Progress in adding renewable energy to the US energy mix, however, was exceedingly slow. By 1995 the main renewable energy source was hydroelectric (still the largest today), while geothermal, wind, and solar accounted for less than half of 1 percent of the US energy supply. The nation was still dependent on fossil fuels for 90 percent of its energy needs.

To speed along the development of renewable energy technology, the federal government adopted regulations to discourage fossil fuel use and encourage alternatives. In 2007, for example, the US Congress passed the Energy Independence and Security Act, which was signed into law by George W. Bush. This law introduced the first increase in fuel economy standards for automobiles since 1975. Basically, the government was telling automobile manufacturers to make more fuel-efficient cars, ones that could be driven for more miles on fewer gallons of gas. The law also rewarded states for the production of renewable fuel sources such as biofuels that used plant matter to make an alternative to gasoline.

At Cross-Purposes

Negotiations in Congress over the 2007 Energy Independence and Security Act, however, revealed one of the thorniest problems in US energy policy. The question of energy independence—not relying on imported oil supplies from the Middle East and other volatile regions—sometimes clashes with the desire to reduce greenhouse gases by increasing the use of renewable energy. If renewable energy could supply all of the US energy needs, then the United States would achieve energy independence and a reduction in greenhouse gases and pollution. Since renewable energy sources, however, are not yet able to do that, energy independence advocates generally argue for increased production

President George W. Bush signs the Energy Independence and Security Act in 2007. The law included the first congressional increase in vehicle fuel economy standards in thirty-two years.

of domestic fossil fuels—energy sources that continue to add to global warming.

Addressing global warming and achieving energy independence, it turns out, are very different priorities. Ideally, technology will someday solve both problems, but until then politicians in the United States are often forced to choose between these priorities. The 2007 Energy Independence and Security Act, for example, originally required all US utility companies to produce 15 percent of their power from renewable energy sources. The intent was to speed up the development and use of renewable energy sources. To pay for the higher costs of producing renewable energy, the law called for the end of tax breaks for oil and gas companies, which are highly profitable even without help from the government. Politicians more worried about energy independence than the environment, however, argued that if the goal were solely to reduce foreign imports, then the US government should continue to support

The Ups and Downs of a Solar White House

When Jimmy Carter installed solar panels on the roof of the White House, he mentioned a similar advancement introduced by the twenty-third president of the United States, Benjamin Harrison. In a symbolic display, Harrison had installed electric lighting in the White House in 1891. The act was meant to demonstrate the potential for new technologies to improve life in the United States.

Carter engaged in his own symbolic act of technological optimism in 1979 when he unveiled solar panels that would help heat the White House's water supply. Although some people thought the historic building should be left as it was, Carter disagreed. He believed that his job as president was to set an example for the public, and he had just called for the expansion of solar power for private homes across the country.

The experiment was short lived, however. When Ronald Reagan succeeded Carter as president in 1981, he ordered the removal of the panels, which were taken off the building in 1986. Nearly three decades later, a new president, Barack Obama, presided over the unveiling of a new generation of solar panels as public endorsement for the US solar sector, which has been growing rapidly.

oil and gas companies and expand drilling in the United States. And that is exactly what happened.

Oil Boom

When Barack Obama was elected president in 2008, environmentalists felt that they had gained an ally in the White House. Obama was a strong supporter of renewable energy. In his 2009 inaugural address, he pointed out, like so many presidents before him, the dangers of an energy policy reliant on imported oil and the burning of fossil fuels. "Each day," he said, "brings further evidence that the ways we use energy strengthen our adversaries and threaten our planet."[16]

Obama was attempting to prioritize climate change over energy security. And then, in the months and years that followed, something remarkable happened—America rediscovered oil. Since US oil production had peaked in 1970, domestic oil production had declined rapidly. There was still oil in the United States, but it was located in harder-to-reach places, and that meant that it would be more expensive to pump out of the ground.

So what happened to reverse the trend? The most important change was the price of oil. While older oil fields in the United States and other countries were producing less oil, demand was still going up. Major economies such as the United States and Japan were consuming more oil than ever before. And developing nations with booming economies, in particular China, were also clamoring for more oil to fuel their own growth. This sharp rise in global demand resulted in a sharp rise in the price of oil. In 2008, for example, the year Obama was elected, oil topped $140 per barrel, a historic high.

This higher price meant that extracting oil from hard-to-reach deposits could be profitable. As a result, oil production in the United States boomed. While high prices provided the motivation for US companies to increase oil drilling, advances in drilling technology provided new methods for extracting oil. State-of-the-art deepwater drilling platforms allowed companies to sink wells in the seafloor beneath deep waters in the Gulf of Mexico. On land, a new process known as hydraulic fracturing, or fracking, allowed oil companies to extract hard-to-reach oil deposits by blasting water or liquefied chemicals into the earth to flush the oil to the surface.

fracking

Using pressurized water and chemicals to force buried oil and natural gas deposits to the earth's surface.

Since Obama took office, oil production has increased by 75 percent. US production has swung up so much that it is now near peak production levels not seen since the 1970s. Although environmentalists oppose the rapid boom in US fossil-fuel production, energy security advocates are celebrating. In 2013 the United States reached an energy independence milestone—the nation produced more oil than it imported. The United States, in fact, has overtaken Saudi Arabia and Russia in production and is now the world's largest oil producer.

Demonstrators who oppose hydraulic fracturing, or fracking, march in Albany, New York. Objections to fracking may be fueling advances in renewable energy.

"This wasn't how energy independence was supposed to look," argues Loren Steffy in *Forbes* magazine. "For decades, the U.S. has pursued alternatives to conventional energy sources as the means of breaking OPEC's [Organization of Petroleum Exporting Countries'] grip on our economy. Instead, we have found that the most effective tool in reducing foreign imports is also the most obvious: increased domestic production."[17]

The States Weigh In

Energy independence has clearly overshadowed environmental concerns in recent years. But all the old problems with oil remain. The supplies will eventually run dry again, though no one is quite sure when. And there are new problems, too. Major public opposition to fracking, which can contaminate groundwater with chemicals and in some cases trigger earthquakes, makes the future of this new method uncertain.

As a result of environmental concerns and the uncertainty surrounding the future of domestic oil production, renewable energy research is also advancing quickly. In part this is because of government regulations requiring alternatives to fossil fuels. But these rules were mandated not from the federal government but from the states. At least thirty-five states now require a certain percentage of electricity to be produced from renewable sources.

Addressing energy concerns locally also allows states to make use of the renewable sources—wind, solar, geothermal, biomass—that fit their particular geographic circumstances. In the Southwest solar energy is a favored alternative because of the abundant sunshine and the open spaces needed for solar farms. New Mexico, for example, has mandated that renewable energy sources provide 20 percent of its electricity supplies by 2020. California is aiming for even greater renewable expansion, mandating 33 percent by 2020.

biomass

Organic matter, such as plant and animal waste, that is used as fuel.

The federal government might strengthen national mandates at some point or adopt further policies to reduce greenhouse gas emissions. In the meantime, Congress and the White House will continue to balance the desire for cheap natural gas, coal, and oil against the desire to reduce the greenhouse gases released during the burning of these fuels. Richard A. Muller, a professor of physics at the University of California–Berkeley, describes these difficult policy choices in an intriguing 2012 book called *Energy for Future Presidents*, in which he provides an energy primer for future White House aspirants. "Your greatest energy challenge," he writes, "will be striking a balance between global warming and energy security."[18]

Renewables Go Mainstream

Focus Questions

1. In your opinion, is some level of pollution acceptable if it allows for cheap fuel for cars and cheap electricity for everyday use? Explain your answer.
2. Since renewable energy costs drop as more consumers use it, should the government provide subsidies to help speed up the spread of renewable technologies? Why or why not?
3. Would you be willing to pay higher costs for energy that does not contribute to global warming? Why or why not?

"I've been an oilman all my life. But this is one emergency we can't drill our way out of."

—T. Boone Pickens, oilman turned wind entrepreneur.

Quoted in *Economist*, "Wind Power: Turbine Time," July 17, 2008. www.economist .com.

For all the excitement generated by renewable energy in the 1970s, the trend was short lived. Domestic drilling for oil and digging for coal remained cheaper alternatives to renewable energy sources like wind and solar. Companies that had jumped into the alternative energy market with the enthusiasm of early oil prospectors found themselves unable to make a profit. Like the early enthusiasm for solar calculators and solar watches, solar companies faded in appeal. "The 'rays of hope' for solar power dimmed," writes Daniel Yergin, "at least in the United States, into a very faint glow."[19]

The reliance on fossil fuels, however, continued to have the same fundamental problems that had prompted interest in solar energy in the 1970s and still remain true today—supplies are limited and often come from places that are unfriendly to the United States. These facts ensured that interest in renewable energy did not disappear altogether. Interest in renewable energy, moreover, has been rekindled in part because energy independence has proved elusive without alternative sources of energy.

Web of Oil

Energy independence, it turns out, is something of a misnomer. The broad term seems to suggest that the United States is short of domestic energy supplies. But this is not exactly the case. "The security problem comes not from an energy shortage (we have plenty), but from an oil shortage—more precisely, from the growing gap between domestic petroleum production rate and the demand for gasoline, diesel, and jet fuel,"[20] explains physicist Richard A. Muller.

The recent boom in offshore drilling and fracking has indeed resulted in a surge in domestic oil and natural gas supplies. But increasing domestic production failed to solve one fundamental fact about the oil market—namely, that it is a global market. It turns out that oil producers and consumers around the world are connected. Changes in production or consumption anywhere in the world affect prices everywhere. "There's no such thing as 'true' oil independence," explains Brad Plumer in the *Washington Post*. "Oil is traded on the world market. If tensions in the Middle East cause prices to spike, everyone is affected, regardless of where they get their crude [oil]." He notes that Canada, as an exporter of oil, is already energy independent by the definition that the United States is using. "But gasoline prices in Canada still rise and fall in accordance with world events, just as they do in the United States or Japan or Europe,"[21] Plumer notes.

Because of the global nature of the oil market, the same oil producers that used oil as a weapon against the United States in the 1970s will continue to have leverage over the US energy sector even if the United States buys less from those suppliers. An example of this occurred just recently. When oil dropped below fifty dollars a barrel in January 2015, the Organization of Petroleum Exporting Countries (OPEC), led by Saudi Arabia, refused to cut output to bring prices back up, even though some OPEC members were losing money by selling oil so cheaply. What could be the motivation for OPEC's coordinated cheap oil policy? It turns out that it was intended to slow down oil drilling in the United States. US oil companies simply cannot turn a profit at prices that low. So during a time of soaring US oil output, oil was once again being used as leverage over the US economy by foreign producers.

nuclear proliferation

The spreading of nuclear weapons, or the technology to make them, to countries that do not already possess the technology.

In fact, four decades after Americans lined up at gas pumps and started to pay attention to their personal connection to world oil markets, the problem remains unresolved. "America's dependence on oil is one of the most serious threats that our nation has faced," Barack Obama said when he unveiled his own plan for energy independence in 2009. "It bankrolls dictators, pays for nuclear proliferation and funds both sides of our struggle against terrorism."[22]

A Texas Oilman Goes Green

Obama's statement was, of course, nothing new. The same argument had been made since the years of the Carter presidency. In those intervening years, however, Americans had fought two wars in oil-rich Iraq and grown more concerned about climate change. Under Obama, renewable energy once again found favor with policy makers in Washington, DC. This renewed interest also met with another welcome new trend. Unlike the 1970s, prices for solar and wind were plummeting. Innovations in wind and solar meant that US manufacturers could compete with fossil fuels on a price basis.

Not only did public opinion once again swing in favor of renewable sources of energy, but investors discovered that wind and solar had become so competitive with fossil fuels that they

T. Boone Pickens, founder of one of the most successful independent oil companies in America, is a strong supporter of renewable energy. He has invested heavily in wind power.

could turn a profit. Renewable energy had always been of interest to politicians, scientists, and environmentalists. But suddenly it found supporters among profit-obsessed businesspeople who had once spent their careers promoting oil or coal. There is perhaps no better example of this surprising trend than the case of T. Boone Pickens.

After earning a degree in geology, Pickens founded one of the most successful independent oil companies in America, Mesa Petroleum. He then spent most of his career using his tenacity to take over other oil companies. His height, swagger, and East Texas accent are perfectly suited to the image of an oilman as presented by Hollywood. True to this type, Pickens is also known for blunt talk and big plans. In 2008 he released his own plan to end the US reliance on foreign oil by increasing domestic production of natural gas as a temporary measure while heavily investing in renewable energy sources, especially wind. "America's dependence

The Legacy of an Oil Fortune

At age sixteen John D. Rockefeller started his first full-time job—as a clerk at a company that sold grain and other commodities. At an even younger age, he had sold candy and raised turkeys to drum up money. But it was the single commodity of oil that would forever be associated with his legacy. Before his twenty-fifth birthday, Rockefeller had pooled his savings with friends and invested in an oil refinery in Cleveland, Ohio, which soon became the Standard Oil Company. Thereafter, he set out to buy up America's other budding refineries. Eventually, he owned a monopoly on oil refining that forced the government to break up his company in 1911.

But before the government broke up the Standard Oil Company, oil made Rockefeller the richest man in the world. Later in his life he donated much of his wealth to various educational and medical causes. To this day Rockefeller's wealth, managed by descendants, flows into different charitable causes. In September 2014, when activists, scientists, and world leaders gathered in New York to discuss climate change, the Rockefeller family announced it would no longer invest in fossil fuels. The symbolic gesture reflected the growing acceptance of the dangers of global warming, even in America's most famous oil family.

on OPEC oil forms the intersection of the three most critical issues America currently faces: the economy, the environment, and our national security,"[23] he said.

Environmentalists, not quite believing their ears, welcomed the oilman's enthusiasm for renewable energy. "It's a good thing we have an oilman saying we can't drill our way out of this problem,"[24] says Dave Hamilton, director for global warming and energy projects at the Sierra Club.

Following the Money

Using Pickens as a bellwether for renewable energy's entry into mainstream American life makes sense when you look at his motivation. "Money! First thing, it's about money,"[25] he says with his characteristic candor. Pickens backed up his ambitious plan to help America break its dependence on fossil fuels by investing heavily in wind farms. He purchased six hundred massive wind-mills and planned to quadruple that number. And then, when the economy crashed in 2008, his plans began to unravel.

The economic slowdown triggered in 2008 and the subsequent glut of oil and natural gas discoveries caused interest in wind energy to falter. It looked like a repeat of the 1970s' fading burst of interest in solar—an ever-unfulfilled dream of cheap, renewable energy. But this time widespread enthusiasm for renewable energy continued despite the competition from cheap oil and gas.

Electricity generated by renewable energy sources climbed steadily. From 2009 to 2013 wind energy accounted for 31 percent of all new capacities for generating electricity. There are now more than forty-eight thousand wind turbines spinning out electricity in the United States. Texas and California, both leading oil producers in the past, have led the way in installing wind capacity, and thirty-nine states now have wind installations adding to local electricity supplies.

Wind energy still accounted for only 4 percent of the total US electricity supply in 2014, but the capacity is expanding quickly because of unrelenting interest from investors. Texas topped 10 percent wind-powered electricity in 2014, and there is a mad rush to build more wind turbines because of growing profits. Pickens, who had been so good at predicting oil markets, still believes he was right to back wind, but he also admits that his timing was off. "I was too early,"[26] he says.

Corporate Embrace

Pickens had always been a maverick, but in this case he was just part of a herd heading in the same direction. Interest in renewable energy has soared in corporate America. Much of this interest is driven by the fact that prices for renewable energy continue to drop. "The cost of providing electricity from wind and solar power plants has plummeted over the last five years," wrote journalist Diane Cardwell in 2014, "so much so that in some markets renewable generation is now cheaper than coal or natural gas."[27]

Major US companies have taken note of the price changes. Walmart, for example, decided that it could decrease its electricity costs on its giant warehouse-like stores by installing solar panels on the roofs in sunnier locations. By 2014 Walmart's solar capacity had reached 105 megawatts, which is more than the solar energy generated by thirty-five states. And the company is hoping to double that output by 2020. Other large retail companies, like Kohl's and Costco, have followed suit. "The price of solar cells is plummeting, and as a result, interest in solar is surging,"[28] writes Richard A. Muller.

megawatt

A unit of power equal to 1 million watts. A watt, named for Scottish engineer James Watt, is the international standard measurement for energy.

The price drop in solar panels is, in part, the result of a self-reinforcing trend. As states have required the expansion of electricity generation from renewable energy, solar panel makers have gained more customers. As business expanded, prices dropped because mass production reduced costs. The profitability of solar companies also results in more money to reinvest in better solar panels — panels that can convert even more of the sun's energy directly into electricity.

The solar industry in the 1970s moved in fits and starts before grinding to a standstill. Prices were high, demand was low, and electricity generation was limited. Now the industry is moving at high speed. "Today, the list of companies moving to clean, affordable solar energy reads like a 'Who's Who' of the most successful corporations in America," says Rhone Resch, who writes about renewable energy. "Simply put, these iconic brands are leading the way when it comes to efforts to transition to clean, renewable energy."[29]

Lingering Opposition

Despite the spike in support for renewable energy in society as a whole, pockets of resistance can still be found at local levels. The building of new hydroelectric dams in the United States, for example, is highly controversial because of the effects on local wildlife and nearby human communities.

Windmills, too, have their opponents. The way that large windmills alter the landscape has upset some local communities. In Cape Cod, Massachusetts, for example, developers of

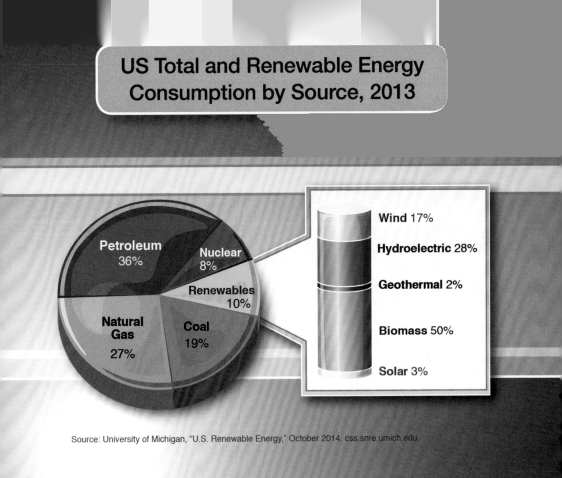

US Total and Renewable Energy Consumption by Source, 2013

Petroleum 36%

Nuclear 8%

Renewables 10%

Natural Gas 27%

Coal 19%

Wind 17%

Hydroelectric 28%

Geothermal 2%

Biomass 50%

Solar 3%

Source: University of Michigan, "U.S. Renewable Energy," October 2014. css.snre.umich.edu.

what would have been the first offshore wind farm in the United States faced stiff public opposition. Environmentalists claimed that the plan to install 130 wind turbines in Nantucket Sound would harm the ecology of Horseshoe Shoal. But the area also sits just off the coast of one of America's most famous vacation islands—Nantucket. Some residents from Nantucket, the larger island of Martha's Vineyard, and coastal Cape Cod, feared that the wind farm would mar the skyline.

This type of opposition, sometimes called "not in my backyard," or NIMBY, opposition, was first made famous by environmentally minded activists opposing the construction of waste dumps, nuclear facilities, oil refineries, and other environmental hazards. Opponents of the Cape Cod wind farm employed the tried-and-true methods of community activism by pressuring local officials to stop the project and drumming up public support for their campaign. As of early 2015 the wind farm's fate was uncertain. Local opposition might well permanently shut down the project.

Similarly, in Texas, where windmills have been planted in huge numbers, some residents have campaigned against new installations because they dislike looking at the giant spinning structures. Even T. Boone Pickens, despite his enthusiasm for wind energy, has said that he would prefer to locate wind turbines on other people's land so that he does not have to look at them. Yet others argue that they are not much different from the oil wells that once dominated the skyline. "Texas has been looking at oil and gas rigs for 100 years, and frankly, wind turbines look a little nicer,"[30] says Jerry Patterson, the Texas land commissioner.

The Environment Strikes Back

Despite the pockets of opposition to particular projects, neither wind farms nor other types of renewable energy are likely to be abandoned as they were in the 1980s. It is not just corporations that have warmed to renewable energy. The public is overwhelmingly supportive. A Gallup poll conducted in 2013 indicated strong public support for the further development of renewable energy. It showed, in particular, that more than 70 percent of all Americans support wind and solar energy expansion, while only 31 percent are supportive of expanding coal mining.

Widespread public support for renewable energy is being driven largely by concerns over the effect of fossil fuels on the environment. When the modern environmental movement kicked off in the 1970s, it focused chiefly on pollution, and great strides have been made to clean polluted air and water in the subsequent decades. The burning of fossil fuels, however, has led to a different environmental problem—the slow heating of the earth's atmosphere, known as global warming.

A Renewable Milestone

In September 2014 Vermont's Burlington Electric Department announced a milestone for the state's largest city, population forty-two thousand. For the first time, the department said, renewable energy sources provided 100 percent of Burlington's electricity. Critics immediately cried foul. They pointed out that the energy was not coming solely from renewable sources at all times. And this was true.

Burlington Electric relies on a number of renewable sources that are not powered up all the time. Windmill output drops on still days, just as solar panels power down when night falls. But the utility company was producing a total electric output that could power all of its electric needs over the course of the year, though particular days might rely on fossil-fuel-generated backup supplies.

Critics also noted that scrap wood (a type of biomass, in the lexicon of renewable energy) burned in an incinerator contributed 35 percent of the electricity. While burning wood releases pollutants, it is considered carbon neutral because when burned, it releases only the carbon that it withdrew from the atmosphere when it was growing. So it is in fact considered a renewable energy resource.

Aside from biomass, the remainder of Burlington's electricity was produced from wind, solar, and hydroelectric generators. Not only was the electricity renewable, but importantly it was also affordable. Residents have not seen an electricity price increase since 2009. "It shows that we're able to do it, and we're able to do it cost effectively," says Christopher Recchia, commissioner of the Vermont Department of Public Service.

Quoted in Wilson Ring, "100% of Power for Vermont City Now Renewable," *Boston Globe*, September 15, 2014. www.bostonglobe.com.

Global warming as a popular environmental issue is a fairly new phenomenon. It was only in 1998 that a team of climatologists released a study of the earth's surface temperature over the past one thousand years. The graph captured the public imagination because of its simple, dramatic illustration of a spike in temperatures that corresponded directly with human activity. The dramatic rise begins in the mid-nineteenth century when fossil fuels began powering the machines of the Industrial Revolution.

The graph continues sharply upward to the present day, reflecting the continuous expansion of industry and the greater consumption of fossil fuels.

The graph and its implications ignited a firestorm of criticism. Could humans really be heating the atmosphere by burning fossil fuels? Fossil-fuel producers certainly resisted the idea. So did their political supporters. Others argued that to abandon fossil fuels would lead to massive job losses and a slower American economy. Some people simply suspected that the warming pattern was just another of the earth's many temperature changes over history.

By 2005, however, scientists from around the world had reached a clear consensus—human activity was contributing to global warming. It was the release of greenhouse gases, such as carbon dioxide (CO_2) and methane, in particular, that was trapping heat inside the earth's atmosphere. Scientists are skeptical as a matter of professional training, and numerous climatologists have run tests to confirm this potentially earth-changing finding.

climatologist
A scientist who studies the earth's climate, especially the long-term variations in climatic conditions such as air and ocean temperatures.

One of those scientists was Richard A. Muller, a physics professor at the University of California–Berkeley. Muller wanted to test the correlation between human activity and global warming through his own research to see if such an important conclusion was indeed correct. He focused in particular on the correlation between the greenhouse gas CO_2 and temperature changes. "The exquisite agreement between the warming and CO_2 suggests that most—maybe all—of the warming of the past 250 years was caused by humans," he writes. "That's a remarkable conclusion for someone (me) who had been stigmatized as a skeptic by the media."[31]

Frightening Scenarios

A mild rising of the earth's temperatures might not seem entirely bad. Humans have adjusted to different climates throughout human history. While hot, arid places would become even hotter, many cooler northern places would have milder winters. So what is the big deal? It turns out that a rise of just 3.6°F (2°C) could fundamentally alter the climate, according to climatologists. The rising temperatures could melt polar ice caps, causing oceans to rise and flood coastal areas. The heating of the ocean could also unleash devastating hurricanes and longer heat waves that could result in droughts and shriveled crops. In 2015 an international team of scientists concluded that global warming doubles the risk of extreme weather. They argued that storms would become more common in both the summer and the winter, with hurricanes and blizzards striking more often and packing a more powerful punch. They described these super storms as "devastating weather events with profound socio-economic consequences."[32]

Scientists, however, are only just beginning to understand the exact relationship between climate change and weather patterns. Although concern over global warming often pops up in conversations on hot, sticky days, local weather is not a good indicator of global temperature changes. Temperatures fluctuate from year to

Shriveled and malformed ears of corn were a common sight in fields in Iowa (pictured) and across the Midwest in 2012. Scientists say that climate change doubles the risk of extreme weather such as drought, hurricanes, and blizzards.

year, and a hot spell in one place on the earth is not a good indicator of a warming planet. Nonetheless, the idea of global warming has entered the popular imagination. A 2013 study by Yale University found that two-thirds of Americans believe that the climate is changing, and at least half the population is worried about the consequences.

The popular acceptance of climate change, in fact, does much to explain the widespread support for renewable energy. Even T. Boone Pickens, who got into wind farming not for the environment but for the profits, thinks it is better to be safe than sorry when it comes to human-made climate change. "I don't want to wait around until the house burns down 'til I decide whether it's a serious fire or not,"[33] says Pickens.

Sharing a
Warmer Planet

Focus Questions

1. Should older, more advanced economies bear a greater responsibility for fighting climate change because they have released more greenhouse gases? Why or why not?
2. Can climate change be stopped without binding agreements among world governments? Why or why not?
3. Should richer countries pay for poorer countries to switch to cleaner energy sources? Explain your answer.

"Climate change cannot be solved at the national level alone."

—Mary Robinson, former president of Ireland and climate activist.

Mary Robinson, "International Cooperation on Global Warming Is Vital to Climate Justice," *New York Times*, September 30, 2014. www.nytimes.com.

Global warming has injected a new urgency in the race for cleaner fuels. Domestic energy security will mean little if climate change results in higher sea levels that swamp cities in the coastal United States. Nor is it possible for the United States to address this problem on its own. The risks posed to the United States by global warming can be addressed only by coordinating efforts to reduce greenhouse gases with countries around the globe. The effects of climate change simply do not recognize nation-

Climate Roundtable

When countries try to coordinate policies on international issues, like climate change, they sometimes meet one on one in what is referred to as a bilateral meeting. Such meetings can help hammer out deals between major powers. The US-China agreement to decrease CO_2 emissions in 2014 is an example of this kind of bilateral diplomacy.

But what if nations want to coordinate policy on a global level? This is generally where the United Nations comes in. The body, headquartered in New York, attempts to give representatives from all nations an equal voice through the meeting of an international forum known as the UN General Assembly. To address specific problems, the United Nations often establishes smaller working groups to coordinate international cooperation.

In 1988 the United Nations established a permanent working group to address climate change. This body is known as the Intergovernmental Panel on Climate Change (IPCC). The body invites scientists from all over the world to review climate data. The IPCC then releases reports summing up those findings. This approach is intended to provide transparent, fact-based research that can be used by the global community to inform the policies of individual nations.

The IPCC has become the most influential single source for climate change research conducted around the globe. "When people say that there is a 'consensus' on global warming," writes physicist Richard A. Muller, "it is the IPCC they're referring to."

Richard A. Muller, *Energy for Future Presidents: The Science Behind the Headlines.* New York: Norton, 2012, p. 40.

al boundaries. "The U.S. must consider the risks that the energy landscape poses to the global climate," argues Bruce Jones of the Brookings Institution, a think tank in Washington, DC. "While the pollution that now clogs cities in China—and increasingly India and Korea—is felt first and foremost locally, its cause—the burning of vast quantities of carbon-based fuels—has global impacts on the climate. And Chinese pollution is already affecting air quality on the West Coast of the United States."[34]

Heating the Greenhouse

Understanding the causes of climate change requires a closer look at the release of greenhouse gases from a historical point of view. The story begins in Europe in the nineteenth century, when coal-fired power plants belched out black smoke that darkened skies and pumped carbon into the atmosphere. Europe was quickly joined by the United States, whose industrial might eventually outstripped Europe's. This breakneck growth marched hand in hand with a more dubious achievement. The United States became the world's leading producer of greenhouse gases.

Because greenhouse gases linger in the atmosphere for generations, the cumulative effect is important. Greenhouse gases released into the atmosphere in the nineteenth century are still contributing to global warming today. To chart the history of emissions, the World Resources Institute, an international research organization, tracks cumulative emissions by country. These figures reveal that between 1850 and 2007, the United States released more CO_2 emissions than the total emissions of the next three highest greenhouse gas–emitting countries combined. The institute calculates, in fact, that the United States is responsible for 28.8 percent of CO_2 emissions during those years.

industrialization

The process by which an economy shifts from a reliance on agriculture to a reliance on the manufacture of modern industrial products in factories.

But the march of industrialization did not stop after it spread throughout Europe and crossed the Atlantic Ocean to the United States. Industrialization has continued to spread all over the globe, and today great swaths of the earth are churning out dangerous emissions as a result of economic development in new regions of the globe. The spread of industrialization is a story of dramatic positives and negatives. Economic growth in India and China, for example, has lifted millions and millions of people out of poverty. But along with the benefits came the harmful environmental effects of using fossil fuels to power growth.

Today cars choke China's roads. Air and water pollution are severe. Some Chinese cities resemble the most polluted European cities during the Industrial Revolution, with buildings blackened by soot and air so polluted that it burns the eyes and throat. Despite demands for a cleaner environment from Chinese citizens, the Chinese government in recent decades has been reluctant to slow industrial growth. Prosperity appears to have trumped environmental concerns in the early decades of China's rapid industrialization.

The Danger Spreads

The spread of industrial growth around the globe in recent decades also dramatically increased the emission of greenhouse gases. Two new trends (one postitive and one negative) in greenhouse gas emissions are in fact happening at the same time. While advanced industrial economies have been reducing harmful emissions, newly industrialized countries have been emitting even more greenhouse gases.

In the United States, for example, emissions of CO_2 had risen for decades. But in 2007 the trend started to reverse. Emissions began to fall. By 2013 US greenhouse gas emissions had hit their lowest point since 1994. The cause of the emissions drop could be

Cars jam a Beijing highway that is shrouded in a thick layer of smog. In recent decades the Chinese government has placed more emphasis on industrialization and prosperity than on environmental concerns.

found in the changing nature of electric power plants. Renewable sources of energy, mostly wind and solar, combined with natural gas were increasingly generating electricity, while coal use was declining. Wind and solar release no greenhouse gases, and natural gas releases only half as much CO_2 as coal when it is burned.

Emissions have been falling in other advanced economies as well, such as those in Europe. But while emissions are falling in some places, they are rising even faster in others. "The global-warming problem derives primarily from rapidly growing coal use in the developing world,"[35] notes Richard A. Muller.

In 2006 China surpassed the United States for the first time in greenhouse gas emissions. Fueled by coal-fired electricity plants and breakneck economic growth, Chinese emissions continued to grow. In 2011 the Netherlands Environmental Assessment Agency found that China accounted for 28.6 percent of all CO_2 emissions. The second-largest polluter was the United States, which was still contributing 16 percent despite a steady decline since 2007.

Perhaps a more remarkable statistic is China's high percentage of historical emissions, measured between 1850 and 2007. According to the World Resources Institute, China has contributed 9 percent of global carbon emissions. What is so remarkable about this figure is the short time during which those emissions actually accumulated. The majority of those CO_2 emissions have been released only in the past few decades. In other words, China is emitting greenhouse gases at an alarming rate, even though it has not been doing so for nearly as long as older industrialized countries.

emerging economies

Countries, including China, India, and Brazil, that are growing in influence because their economies have grown swiftly in the past few decades, generally through rapid industrialization.

More troubling still is that energy demands are continuing to rise all over the developing world. According to the 2014 *BP Statistical Review of World Energy*, an annual report by oil and gas giant BP, "Emerging economies continue to dominate global energy demand, accounting for 80% of growth last year and nearly 100% over the past decade."[36]

Accelerated Development

The developing world's rapid climb up the ranks of global polluters reflects this accelerated industrialization. Whereas industrial development took countries in Europe and the United States more than a century, rapidly industrializing countries like China have replicated the process in a matter of a few decades.

Since China's rising economy occurred at a time of increased concern over global warming, the international community has been sharply critical of the expansion of fossil-fuel burning in developing economies. But China and other developing nations bristle when they are pressured to reduce emissions. They point out that the West has been polluting for much longer and that the United States still releases more greenhouse gases per person than heavily populated China. The Chinese have also argued that much of their industrial energy use powers factories that pump out consumer products for Western markets. "All the West has done is export a great slice of its carbon footprint to China and make China the world's factory,"[37] says Yang Ailun of the environmental group Greenpeace.

This debate over who is responsible for fossil-fuel emissions has resulted in the regular exchange of barbs between US and Chinese leaders. When world leaders gathered in Kyoto, Japan, in 1997 to hammer out a plan to reduce greenhouse gas emissions, the United States criticized the final agreement. That agreement, known as the Kyoto Protocol, was opposed by the United States because it exempted developing economies, such as China and India, from reducing emissions. US president George W. Bush reasoned that if the United States had to cut emissions, so should the nations that account for recent increases in greenhouse gases.

The United States ultimately refused to sign the agreement, and it appeared that there was little chance of further agreement between the world's two largest polluters. Neither country wanted to restrict economic growth in its own country (by reducing emissions) in a way that might benefit the other. It appeared to be a standoff, and emissions continued to climb.

But the situation in China was quickly changing. Breakneck development had made China's leaders increasingly worried about polluted air, contaminated and dying rivers, and global warming.

Saharan Solar Power

Increasingly, renewable energy supplies are being looked at without regard for national boundaries. Reducing dependency on fossil fuels might well require the harnessing of renewable sources wherever they make the most sense. This means creating wind farms in the windiest places, such as Great Britain's coastal waters, and placing solar installations in areas of unrelenting sunshine.

One of those sunny places is North Africa's Sahara Desert. But what good is energy for human activity when it is generated in a sparsely inhabited desert? The answer is that it can function as a valuable export commodity. Solar energy installations can produce local jobs and revenue for North African governments while supplying electricity to more densely populated Europe through transmission lines that would run under the Mediterranean Sea.

Renewable energy companies are already at work on such projects. The TuNur project hopes to capture solar energy in the North African country of Tunisia and transmit it to Italy, just across the Mediterranean. Moreover, the project is designed to concentrate the sun's energy during the day to heat molten salt. At night water is channeled through the heated salt, which releases steam as the water vaporizes. The steam is used to turn electricity-producing turbines during the night. This method offers one solution to solar energy's peskiest problem—its inability to generate energy at night. Or, as one team of investment advisors put it, "Voilà, solar power in the dark!"

Commodities Research Team, "Saharan Solar Power Opens Energy Corridor to Europe," *Wall Street Daily,* October 29, 2014. www.wallstreetdaily.com.

This came about not because of international pressure but because of the potential for pollution and global warming to harm Chinese citizens, who would then become critics of the government. Chinese advances in renewable energy technology, in fact, accelerated just as remarkably fast as its industrial development had in previous decades. And both China and the United States realized that climate change was potentially ruinous to both countries equally.

In November 2014 US president Barack Obama joined Chinese president Xi Jinping in Beijing, China, for a historic climate agreement. The world's two largest polluters agreed to reduce emissions. It was the first time the Chinese government had ever committed to specific emissions cuts. "It shows what's possible when we work together on an urgent global challenge,"[38] said Obama at the signing ceremony.

Moving Toward Renewables

Both China and the United States, however, are still having trouble weaning themselves off highly polluting coal. But both are working in the same direction. Despite its heavy use of coal, China has, in fact, been investing huge amounts of money into renewable energy sources. As a result, solar and wind capacity have expanded quickly. There are even plans to build solar and wind farms on a scale as massive as the Three Gorges Dam, the world's largest renewable energy power generator.

A look at recent headlines highlights China's rapid drive to expand renewable energy supplies. "China Leads in Renewable Investment Again!" trumpeted *Forbes* magazine in 2014. In early 2015 Fox News ran an article under the headline "China Wind Power Capacity Jumps to Record High as Country Moves to Renewable Energy." The article reported, "Already, China is a world leader in solar and wind energy production and has announced plans to further boost renewable energy investment."[39]

China, in fact, leads the world in renewable energy capacity, but 80 percent of China's energy still comes from highly polluting coal. China burns almost as much coal as the rest of the world combined. For supporters of renewable energy, the rapid investment is encouraging. For those who worry about climate change, the amount of coal being burned is troubling.

Europe's Renewable Embrace

Other countries have had more success replacing fossil fuels with renewable sources of energy. In Europe, which set off the world's large-scale consumption of fossil fuels during the Industrial Revolution, there are now countries spearheading a modern-day renew-

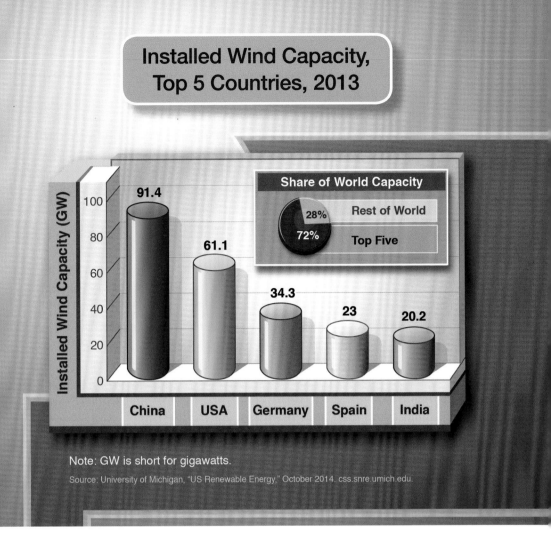

Installed Wind Capacity, Top 5 Countries, 2013

Installed Wind Capacity (GW)

China 91.4
USA 61.1
Germany 34.3
Spain 23
India 20.2

Share of World Capacity

28% Rest of World
72% Top Five

Note: GW is short for gigawatts.

Source: University of Michigan, "US Renewable Energy," October 2014. css.snre.umich.edu.

able revolution. In October 2014 Germany, Europe's largest economy, reached a milestone. For the first time it produced more energy from renewable sources than from any other single energy source. It produced 27.7 percent of its energy needs solely from renewable sources for the first nine months of the year. Germany has been a global leader in the adoption of alternative energy. The country has embarked on an ambitious *Energiewende* (energy transition) policy that aims to move the country away from fossil fuels and phase out nuclear energy by 2022. To reach those goals, the Germans have blanketed rooftops with solar panels in cities and installed giant solar farms in open spaces. Meanwhile, windmills spin across the country both on land and in German coastal waters. "On a drive through eastern Germany, you would have to be blind to not see wind turbines," writes journalist Jennifer Runyon. "They dot the horizon of the relatively flat country in every direction."[40]

Germany has made quick strides in expanding renewable capacity, and it is now shooting for 35 percent renewable energy by 2020 and 65 percent by 2035, one of the most ambitious goals in the world. Solar and wind capacity have shown remarkable potential when conditions are right—when clouds are few and winds strong. On a single spring day in 2014, Germany produced nearly 75 percent of its electricity demand from renewable energy alone. But at present this can only be achieved for brief periods of ideal weather.

Similarly in the United Kingdom, an island nation for which the sea has been vital, wind farms are sprouting up in the windswept coastal waters and capturing powerful wind currents in Scotland. The British generated more than 9 percent of their energy in 2014 by wind power alone, and capacity is still expanding through the addition of new wind farms and the use of improved windmills. In 2010 British prime minister David Cameron pledged that Britain would produce 20 percent of its energy needs from renewable sources by 2020 and cut CO_2 emissions by 80 percent by 2050. European countries are largely in agreement that renewable energy must play a greater role in future energy production all over the Continent.

Coming Up Short

Despite the shared goals of expanding renewable energy supplies, the costs still cause considerable hand-wringing among European leaders. During times of slow economic growth, like that caused by the 2008 recession, shrinking tax revenues strain government budgets, including financial support for renewable energy. In fact, Great Britain is considering dropping subsidies for new onshore wind farms to save taxpayers money. "We now have enough bill-payer-funded onshore wind in the pipeline to meet our renewable energy commitments and there's no requirement for any more,"[41] says Michael Fallon, the British minister of state for energy.

Because some renewable energy sources are still only competitive with fossil fuels when they are subsidized by the government, politicians will continue to face difficult decisions between lower government spending and renewable energy. The political

A sprawling solar farm in Spain illustrates the country's dedication to renewable energy. Spain's early successes with renewable energy efforts have been overshadowed by rising costs and government debt.

risks of backing more expensive energy policies were vividly displayed in another European country—Spain. Until 2010 Spain was a renewable energy success story, much like Germany. In a five-year period alone, from 2007 to 2012, it doubled the amount of renewable energy it produced. The growth of the renewable energy sector, moreover, was creating well-paying jobs. It seemed like a clear success story. But then the problems began. It turned out that the Spanish government was spending more money on renewable energy than it was taking in, resulting in high deficits (or government debts).

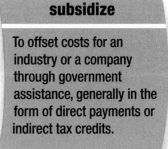

subsidize

To offset costs for an industry or a company through government assistance, generally in the form of direct payments or indirect tax credits.

After the 2008 global recession caused a slowdown in Spain's economic activity, subsidies were cut, and energy costs rose. Citizens unhappy about more expensive energy costs began to turn against renewable energy. "We've gone from misery to ruin,"[42] says

Jaume Margarit, director of the Association of Renewable Energy Producers. Spain's experience highlights the political difficulties for governments trying to switch from fossil fuels to renewable energy sources. If the policies are not well planned, costs can shoot up during times of economic hardship and cause the policies to lose public support. This tricky governmental factor will become less important, however, if the price of renewable energy continues to drop. But for now, cost concerns are slowing the process of replacing fossil fuels with renewable energy sources.

Moreover, energy demands just continue to rise. "Continuing on today's energy path without any change in policies would not only mean that the pressing issue of climate change is not addressed, but also that our dependency on fossil fuels is set to increase," says the European Renewable Energy Council. "We would be bound to unpredictable energy prices, all of which would result in detrimental impacts on Europe's economy and in energy insecurity."[43]

International cooperation will be vital to reducing greenhouse gases and expanding renewable energy technology. But at present, the technology is not ready to fuel 100 percent of the world's energy needs. To completely abandon the practice of burning fossil fuels for energy, scientists will need to come up with imaginative new technologies, perhaps as remarkable as anything found in the pages of science fiction.

Chapter Five

From Science Fiction to Science Fact

Focus Questions

1. Should the government help pay for the costs of new, often expensive, renewable technologies that reduce greenhouse gases and reliance on foreign energy supplies? Why or why not?
2. Do you believe renewable energy technology will replace the burning of fossil fuels for electricity even without the discovery of new technologies? Explain your answer.
3. If scientists in one country learn to harness the sun's energy in space, should that technology be shared with other counties? Why or why not?

"The fact is, a 100 percent renewable energy future is technically feasible."

—Steve Sawyer, Secretary General, Global Wind Energy Council.

Steve Sawyer, "A Renewable Energy Future," *Huffington Post,* September 10, 2014. www.huffingtonpost.com.

Imagine a world in which humans could tap into an unending supply of renewable energy and abandon for good the fossil fuels that produce pollution and contribute to global warming. What if, for example, the heat deep below the surface of the earth could be turned into electricity? What if people could dispose of their garbage by unleashing armies of bacteria that turned solid waste into a form of energy? What if solar panels could be positioned in space where they could capture the sun's energy twenty-four hours a day, uninterrupted by night or cloud cover?

These ideas might sound like science fiction, but all of them are either already in use or currently being developed. High energy prices in recent years and worries over global warming have spurred an explosion of innovation in the search for renewable energy technologies. These factors have unleashed an era of infectious optimism. The excitement arises both from the possibility of expanding proven technologies, such as using the earth's internal heat, and from the possibility of using technology in radically new ways, such as space-based solar stations. These technologies might one day create energy sources as futuristic as those imagined by science-fiction writers.

The Heat Beneath the Earth's Surface

Humans have burned fossil fuels such as oil and coal since the beginning of recorded history to create heat. All the while, those same humans, busying themselves on the earth's surface, have been sitting on top of a bottled-up heat source that resides deep beneath their feet. That heat is called geothermal energy. It was created in part during the earth's formation, a process that trapped energy inside the planet. Geothermal energy is also the result of radioactive decay inside the earth, which releases heat over time. Because of the pressure inside the earth, the heat trapped within seeks to escape to the surface. There are clues to the boiling temperatures below the earth's surface in the form of naturally occurring steam vents hissing from the ground and from bubbling pools of hot water located on the surface. The most dramatic evidence for geothermal energy is found in the towering volcanoes that spew lava after erupting from the pressures below.

The fearsome spectacle of a volcanic eruption makes plain the tremendous heat energy trapped within the planet. When Jules Verne, a French author of adventure stories, dispatched a fictional scientific expedition in his 1864 novel *Journey to the Center of the Earth*, he used an extinct volcano as the expedition's entry point. "It is a mountain five thousand feet high," he wrote, "one of the most remarkable in the world, if its crater leads down to the centre of the Earth."[44]

After descending into the volcano, Verne's adventurers encounter the steamy innards of the earth, which gets hotter and hotter as they near its center, known as the core. As a matter of fact, humans have been using this subterranean heat source since antiquity. The ancient Romans pumped it into their homes for indoor heating. In the nineteenth century, when Verne was writing his fanciful tales, aristocrats from Europe and well-to-do professionals in the United States used geothermal energy to heat pools in luxurious vacation spas intended to restore health and vitality.

Amazing Stories

Science-fiction writers are sometimes called futurists because they create imaginative descriptions of future worlds. From ray guns to space travel, futurists have often dreamed up technologies that did not yet exist. Writing in 1911, for example, Hugo Gernsback described how solar-electric generators, which he called "helio-dynamophores," could provide all of New York's electricity in 2660, the setting of his futuristic novel *Ralph 124C 41+*. Gernsback popularized the science-fiction genre in his quarterly publication *Amazing Stories*. Through the magazine, he inspired the fictional experimentation of other futurists, and to this day awards for excellence in science fiction are called Hugo Awards in his honor.

Science-fiction writers have always been early birds in portraying future technologies, even if they did not know how those technologies would work. The value of thinking beyond the realm of possibility has not been lost on scientists. University of Minnesota physics professor James Kakalios, for example, requires students to delve into the fiction of futurists for inspiration. "Both scientific research and science fiction," he says, "begin with the same two words: 'What if?'"

Quoted in James A. Fussell, "Science Fiction Inspires Innovation in the Real World," Phys.org, October 22, 2013. http://phys.org.

From Spas to Energy Supply

In Northern California's Mayacamas Mountains, for example, the steam rising from the earth's surface was converted into a hot springs resort called the Geysers Resort Hotel in the 1850s. In later years it occurred to scientists that this energy could be exploited on a much greater scale. In fact, the naturally rising steam can be harnessed to turn a turbine that creates electricity. The same principle is used in a coal-burning electrical power station, but the steam heat from geothermal energy releases no greenhouse gases or other pollutants.

While the resort closed in 1978, the Geysers found new purpose as a major source of energy. Today it is the largest geothermal producer of electricity on the planet. According to the company that runs the site, the Geysers can produce enough electricity to supply 725,000 homes and provides 60 percent of the energy needs for an area stretching from the Golden Gate Bridge in San Francisco to the northern border of California. At present, the United States is the world's largest producer of geothermal energy, but it accounted for just 0.41 percent of US energy supplies in 2013, according to the US Energy Information Administration.

A geothermal plant in Iceland transforms the earth's heat into electricity. Innovation is promoting new thinking about the future of geothermal energy.

Geothermal energy has had a more transformative effect on other nations, perhaps none more so than the chilly, volcanic island of Iceland. To find a fictional volcano that might lead into the center of the earth, Jules Verne in fact chose Iceland, long famous for its volcanic activity and steaming pools bubbling up from the rocky landscape. Icelanders long ago learned that they could make use of that heat escaping from the earth to heat their homes. Today geothermal heat is pumped into nine out of ten homes in Iceland, and it accounts for 25 percent of the country's electricity supply.

Innovation is also prompting new thinking about the future of geothermal energy. By drilling farther into the earth, Iceland has the potential to tap even greater supplies of geothermal energy. Iceland might someday export geothermal electricity to continental Europe if undersea cables can connect the supplier with the consumer. "It can change the energy picture in Iceland very dramatically," says Wilfred Elders, a geologist who is working on the project. "And it could make a big impact on the supply of electricity in Northern Europe."[45]

Energy Under the Microscope

Another potential energy source that is of increasing interest to scientists is derived from the invisible organisms that exist all around us and even inside us—bacteria. These microscopic organisms already aid the human body in digesting food and breaking down waste material. Scientists are now experimenting with this digestive process on a giant scale to produce energy.

At the Newtown Creek Wastewater Treatment Plant in Brooklyn, New York, both human waste and food scraps from the ravenous city are being slowly digested by armies of bacteria. The process occurs in giant, futuristic-looking steel eggs, called digester eggs. "The digesters like to be fed like us: three times a day,"[46] says Jimmy Pynn, the plant's superintendent. As the bacteria digest waste material, they

digester

A container used for the decomposition of food scraps or other waste.

release a gas called methane. Methane acts as a harmful greenhouse gas when released into the atmosphere, but when captured it can act as a fuel. In fact, waste-treatment plants using bacteria to gobble up waste generally run on the electricity produced from the methane released in the process. Such waste-treatment plants are growing in number and proving that they can be self-sufficient recyclers, both reducing waste and powering themselves.

Scientists are looking at other ways to use microscopic organisms to produce energy. Scientists at the Massachusetts Institute of Technology, for example, have altered a form of common soil bacteria through a process known as bioengineering. This process altered the diet of the bacteria so that they would consume carbon. When the bacteria overeat, they store food as a fat, just like humans. In this case, however, the fatty substance is isobutanol, which can replace gasoline in combustion engines like those found in cars. In theory these bacteria could be fattened up on carbon-based food, and then harvested as a renewable fuel source. This could potentially replace the need for environmentally harmful fossil fuels

bioengineering

The use of biological techniques, such as changing the genes of an organism, to modify its nature for some particular practical benefit.

A Mazda Le Mans Series race car, powered by the alternative fuel isobutanol, demonstrates the potential of bioengineered fuels. Renewable fuels made this way could provide an alternative to fuels made from oil and gas.

such as oil and gas. In another experiment, scientists have sub-
jected microbes to electric shock treatment, known as electrolysis,
which causes a chemical reaction that turns their CO_2 diet into a
type of fuel. "With nothing more than a jolt of energy, the amazing
microbes create liquid fuel, which is energy-dense and doesn't lose
its charge over time" writes journalist Derek Mead. "It's a development that could potentially change the energy landscape."[47]

Using bacteria and microorganisms to create energy has
proved feasible. But the technology has so far been unable to
reach the scale of production that would be needed for them to
become major contributors to the world's energy needs.

Importing the Sun's Energy

What is evident from recent experiments is that scientists are sift-
ing through a whole spectrum of possibilities for new renewable
energy sources. They are also thinking on a grand scale. One of
the most ambitious of all renewable projects currently in the ex-
perimental phase could radically—and permanently—change the
world's energy supply.

In November 2003 a wispy-haired, lifelong space enthusiast
described a future world in which photovoltaic solar panels installed on the surface of the moon would be used to collect the
sun's energy. That energy would then be beamed back to earth
in the form of electromagnetic radiation, akin to powerful radio
waves. But this was no science-fiction convention. It was a hearing of the US Senate Committee on Commerce, Science, and
Transportation. The speaker was David R. Criswell, a professor
and the director of Space Systems Operations at the University
of Houston. That Criswell was a scientist who had spent his career studying space made his message no less fantastic. Speak-
ing to the audience of politicians, whose job includes addressing
America's energy problems, Criswell noted that by 2050, "solar
power from the Moon could provide everyone clean, affordable,
and sustainable electric power."[48]

Nor was Criswell talking just about Americans. He was in fact
arguing that the energy from the sun alone could provide for the

energy needs of the entire planet—and most important, the sun provides energy that is self-sustaining. "The sun is the ultimate necessary power source for a truly prosperous (large-scale) human society,"[49] he says.

So just what is it that makes collecting the sun's energy in space more attractive than collecting it from the earth? The answer lies in the intensity of extraterrestrial solar radiation. In space there is about ten times as much usable solar energy than on the earth. Two factors account for this. The first is that in space, the sun's energy is unhindered by the earth's atmosphere. As terrestrial solar panels capture the sun's rays, the energy has already been diluted by passing through the gases and other interferences in the atmosphere. This decreases the amount of energy that can be collected from solar panels. The second advantage of collecting solar energy in space is the ability to do away with the night. Solar stations in space could be positioned like satellites orbiting the sun, collecting solar energy all day, every day. No cloudy days or long winter nights would interfere with collection. Space, it would seem, solves the most nettlesome aspects of solar energy collection—cloudy weather and the darkness of night.

electromagnetic radiation

A form of energy resulting from the movement of electrically charged particles through a vacuum, such as space.

Although Criswell's futuristic solution to capturing solar energy sounds fantastic, it relies on science that is already proven. "NASA and the US Department of Energy did a study in the late '70s that cost $20 million at the time and looked at it in pretty great depth," says Paul Jaffe, a spacecraft engineer at the US Naval Research Laboratory. "The conclusion at that time was that there was nothing wrong with the physics but the real question is the economics."[50]

The Case of Japan

That question of economics lies at the heart of debates over all renewable energy supplies. But attitudes toward expenses shift when societies are faced with more threatening problems. The government's interest in promoting cleaner energy has resulted

A solar station in space positioned like a satellite orbiting the sun could collect solar energy day and night. Research on ideas like this one could lead to new sources of renewable energy.

from the twin motives of reducing harmful emissions and achieving energy security. But a third factor is of even greater importance: The government is also responsible for protecting citizens from potential dangers resulting from its own policies.

Nations that rely on nuclear energy, for example, run the risk of losing support if an accident happens. This was certainly the case in Japan in 2011 after an earthquake triggered a tsunami that slammed into a nuclear installation 150 miles (241 km) north of Tokyo, Japan's capital. The violent storm surge damaged the nuclear reactors, which sent radioactive material spewing into the air around the site. The incident caused the public to turn against the nuclear industry, and the government was forced to shut down all of Japan's nuclear reactors while it investigated the fallout.

Nuclear energy, however, provided 26 percent of Japan's total power generation in 2011. It was also Japan's cheapest source of energy. The country has scant supplies of fossil fuels and imports 90 percent of its energy resources. Japan was already the world's largest importer of natural gas, the second-largest coal importer, and the third-largest oil importer. What would it do without its supply

Building a Better Battery

Ever since Italian scientist Alessandro Volta invented the battery in 1800, innovators have been racing to create a better battery. This is because transporting electricity requires a storage unit that can fuel modern inventions such as cell phones and laptop computers. Larger batteries can also store energy from renewable energy installations such as wind turbines and solar panels so that the energy can be used when there is no wind or sun. Despite the intense interest in creating a better battery, breakthroughs have been rare. Even the most modern batteries, such as the lithium ion batteries used in cell phones, run on principles that have been understood for decades.

In 2013 scientists at England's University of East Anglia discovered the possibility of creating a renewable battery from bacteria. The scientists bred bacteria on an electrode, which formed the anode side of a battery, the part that absorbs the energy. "Couple this anode to a cathode, feed the bacteria with carbon-based organic matter, say, from industrial wastewater," writes journalist Sophia Ktori, "and you can construct a microbial fuel cell, or MFC, that generates electricity, albeit in small amounts." The experiment represents one of the ways that scientists are trying to rework the concept of a battery in the hope of finding a reliable way to store greater amounts of portable energy.

Sophia Ktori, "Bio-Batteries: Creating Energy from Bacteria," *Engineering & Technology*, July 15, 2013. http://eandt .theiet.org.

of cheap nuclear energy? "The accident at the Fukushima Daiichi nuclear power plant prompted an exhaustive and systematic search for alternatives," writes Susumu Sasaki of the Japan Aerospace Exploration Agency, "yet Japan lacks both fossil fuel resources and empty land suitable for renewable power installations."[51]

To the Stars and Back

The Japanese government had already been investigating the possibility of launching satellites into space to capture the sun's energy. After the accident at Fukushima, the program gained renewed urgency and increased funding. To make this futuristic idea a reality, Japan's highly advanced space program focused on the question of transmitting stored energy from a space-based solar station back to earth. From the earliest conception of space-based solar power, the transmission question has been the most vexing.

The first description of an extraterrestrial solar station appeared in 1941 in the science-fiction story "Reason" by Isaac Asimov, a scientist made famous by his futuristic writing. In the story, the crew of a space-based solar power station frets over an approaching electron storm that could interfere with the transmitter that beams the sun's radiation to earth. "Deviations in arc of a hundredth of a millisecond—invisible to the naked eye—were enough to send the beam wildly out of focus—enough to blast hundreds of square miles of Earth into incandescent ruin,"[52] Asimov writes.

Asimov's fictional solar station relies on concentrated light—a laser beam—to transmit the solar energy back to earth. Japan's scientists, however, want to make use of microwaves that would be transmitted to receiving antennas on earth in much the same way as radio waves are transmitted. "When laypeople hear these orbital solar farms described, they often ask if it would be safe to send a powerful beam of microwaves down to Earth," notes Sasaki. "Wouldn't it cook whatever's in its path, like food in a microwave oven? Some people have a grisly mental image of roasted seagulls dropping from the sky. In fact, the beam wouldn't even be intense enough to heat your coffee."[53]

Japanese and American scientists have already experimented with beaming energy by microwave between a mountaintop on one Hawaiian island and a volcano on another. In coming years the Japanese plan to conduct transmission trials in space. In the meantime a host of private companies have begun researching the feasibility of private space-based solar collectors.

For now the idea remains a promising dream, somewhere between science fiction and science fact. But the potential to capture a permanent source of renewable energy and solve the problems of pollution, global warming, and energy security continues to drive enthusiasm for extraterrestrial solar stations. "It's going to replace nearly everything else," says Ralph Nansen, a leading proponent of the technology. "I don't think there's any doubt that within the next century we will be getting the majority of our power from space. It's just a question of when."[54]

Introduction: Alternating Currents

1. *New York Times*, "Edison's Electric Light," September 5, 1882, p. 8.
2. Quoted in *Life*, "Thanksgiving and Plenty," November 29, 1954, p. 22.
3. Richard K. Lester and David M. Hart, *Unlocking Energy Innovation: How America Can Build a Low-Cost, Low-Carbon Energy System*. Cambridge, MA: MIT Press, 2012, p. 2.
4. Daniel Yergin, *The Quest: Energy, Security, and the Re-making of the Modern World*. New York: Penguin, 2011, p. 546.

Chapter One: The Rise of Renewable Energy

5. Quoted in Robert W. Righter, *Wind Energy in America: A History*. Norman: Oklahoma University Press, 1996, p. 32.
6. Quoted in American Physical Society, "This Month in Physics History: April 25, 1954; Bell Labs Demonstrates the First Practical Silicon Solar Cell," 2015. www.aps.org.
7. Quoted in Jeremy Hsu, "First Solar-Powered Satellite Still Flying at 50," Space.com, March 18, 2008. www.space.com.
8. Franklin Roosevelt, "Campaign Address in Portland, Oregon on Public Utilities and Development of Hydro-Electric Power," American Presidency Project, September 21, 1932. www.presidency.ucsb.edu.
9. Quoted in National Hydropower Association, "Modernizing Hydropower," 2015. www.hydro.org.

Chapter Two: The Search for Energy Independence

10. Patrick Tyler, *A World of Trouble: The White House and the Middle East—from the Cold War to the War on Terror*. New York: Farrar, Straus and Giroux, 2010, p. 158.
11. Gal Luft and Anne Korin, "The Myth of US Energy Dependence," *Foreign Affairs*, October 15, 2013. www.foreignaffairs.com.

12. Richard Nixon, "Address to the Nation About National Energy Policy," *American Presidency Project*, November 25, 1973. www.presidency.ucsb.edu.

13. Amanda Little, *Power Trip: From Oil Wells to Solar Cells—Our Ride to the Renewable Future*. New York: HarperPerennial, 2009, p. 17.

14. Jimmy Carter, "Solar Energy Remarks Announcing Administration Proposals," *American Presidency Project*, June 20, 1979. www.presidency.ucsb.

15. Robert Rapier, "The Lasting Impact of the 1973 Oil Embargo," *Energy Trends Insider*, October 23, 2013. www.energytrends insider.com.

16. Quoted in *New York Times*, "Barack Obama's Inaugural Address," January 20, 2009. www.nytimes.com.

17. Loren Steffy, "Is This What 'Energy Independence' Is Supposed to Look Like?," *Forbes*, December 1, 2014. www .forbes.com.

18. Richard A. Muller, *Energy for Future Presidents: The Science Between the Headlines*. New York: Norton, 2012, p. 305.

Chapter Three: Renewables Go Mainstream

19. Yergin, *The Quest*, p. 533.

20. Muller, *Energy for Future Presidents*, p. 291.

21. Brad Plumer, "Five Things to Know About Mitt Romney's Energy Plan," *Wonkblog*, *Washington Post*, August 23, 2012. www.washingtonpost.com.

22. Quoted in *Washington Post*, "Obama Announces Plans to Achieve Energy Independence," January 26, 2009. www .washingtonpost.com.

23. T. Boone Pickens, "Pickens Plan," 2015. www.pickensplan .com.

24. Quoted in Steve Hargreaves, "Wind Power: A Reality Check," *CNN Money*, July 31, 2008. http://money.cnn.com.

25. Quoted in David Case, "Texas Oil Tycoon Tackles Renewable Energy," *Fast Company*, June 1, 2008. www.fastcompany .com.

26. Quoted in James Osborne, "Wind Rush: From Panhandle to Gulf Coast, Texas Sees Surge in Wind Energy Projects," *Dallas Morning News*, April 2014. http://res.dallasnews.com.

27. Diane Cardwell, "Solar and Wind Energy Start to Win on Price vs. Conventional Fuels," *New York Times*, November 23, 2014. www.nytimes.com.
28. Muller, *Energy for Future Presidents*, p. 145.
29. Rhone Resch, "New Report Shows Top U.S. Companies Investing Big in Solar," *Renewable Energy World*, October 16, 2013. www.renewableenergyworld.com.
30. Quoted in Clifford Krauss, "Move Over, Oil, There's Money in Texas Wind," *New York Times*, February 23, 2008. www.nytimes.com.
31. Muller, *Energy for Future Presidents*, p. 61.
32. Quoted in Helen Briggs, "Study: Global Warming 'Doubles Risk' of Extreme Weather," BBC News, January 26, 2015. www.bbc.com.
33. Quoted in Case, "Texas Oil Tycoon Tackles Renewable Energy."

Chapter Four: Sharing a Warmer Planet

34. Bruce Jones, "Despite Growing Energy Independence, U.S. Cannot Escape Global Risks," *Planet Policy* (blog), Brookings Institution, May 27, 2014. www.brookings.edu.
35. Muller, *Energy for Future Presidents*, p. 292.
36. BP, *BP Statistical Review of World Energy*, June 2014, p. 1. www.bp.com.
37. Quoted in *Scientific American*, "Is the World Outsourcing Its Greenhouse Emissions to China?," November 5, 2009. www.scientificamerican.com.
38. Quoted in Calum MacLeod and Melanie Eversley, "U.S., China Reach 'Historic' Deal to Cut Emissions," *USA Today*, November 12, 2014. www.usatoday.com.
39. Associated Press, "China Wind Power Capacity Jumps to Record High as Country Moves to Renewable Energy," Fox News, February 12, 2015. www.foxnews.com.
40. Jennifer Runyon, "7 Renewable Energy Lessons from Germany," *Renewable Energy World*, October 3, 2014. www.renewableenergyworld.com.
41. Quoted in Patrick Wintour, "Tories Would Scrap Windfarm Subsidies," *Guardian* (Manchester, UK), April 24, 2014. www.theguardian.com.

42. Quoted in Andrés Cala, "Renewable Energy in Spain Is Taking a Beating," *New York Times*, October 8, 2013. www.nytimes.com.

43. European Renewable Energy Council, "The Future of Renewable Energy," 2012. www.erec.org.

Chapter Five: From Science Fiction to Science Fact

44. Jules Verne, *Journey to the Center of the Earth*. London: Ward, Lock, 1877. www.gutenberg.org.

45. Quoted in Clay Dillow, "Are Volcanoes the Energy Source of the Future?," CNBC, January 5, 2015. www.cnbc.com.

46. Quoted in Joel Rose, "Turning Food Waste into Fuel Takes Gumption and Trillions of Bacteria," *The Salt* (blog), NPR, March 11, 2014. www.npr.org.

47. Derek Mead, "Bacteria That Eat Carbon and Poop Fuel Might Just Save the Planet," *Motherboard* (blog), March 29, 2012. http://motherboard.vice.com.

48. Quoted in Senate Committee on Commerce, Science, and Transportation, "Testimony of Dr. David R. Criswell: Senate Hearing on 'Lunar Exploration,'" SpaceRef, November 6, 2003. www.spaceref.com.

49. Quoted in Sam Dinkin, "Reaping Powerful Ideas from a Luminary," *Space Review*, April 11, 2005. www.thespacereview.com.

50. Quoted in Peter Shadbolt, "Space-Based Solar Power: The Energy of the Future?," CNN, December 18, 2014. www.cnn.com.

51. Susumu Sasaki, "How Japan Plans to Build an Orbital Solar Farm: JAXA Wants to Make the Sci-Fi Idea of Space-Based Solar Power a Reality," *IEEE Spectrum*, April 24, 2014. http://spectrum.ieee.org.

52. Isaac Asimov, "Reason," 1941, Adds Donna. http://addsdonna.com.

53. Sasaki, "How Japan Plans to Build an Orbital Solar Farm."

54. Quoted in Emmet Cole, "Space-Based Solar Farms Power Up," BBC News, February 27, 2013. www.bbc.com.

Books

John Allen, *Thinking Critically: Renewable Energy*. San Diego, CA: ReferencePoint, 2014.

Julie Kerr Casper, *Fossil Fuels and Pollution: The Future of Air Quality*. New York: Facts On File, 2010.

Robert Curley, ed., *Renewable and Alternative Energy*. New York: Britannica, 2012.

Sylvia Engdahl, *Energy Alternatives*. New Haven, CT: Gale, 2015.

Amy Francis, *Wind Farms*. New Haven, CT: Gale, 2015.

Terry Allan Hicks, *The Pros and Cons of Biofuel*. New York: Cavendish Square, 2014.

Philip Jodidio, ed., *100 Contemporary Green Buildings*. Los Angeles: Taschen America, 2013.

Mike Rigsby, *Doable Renewables: 16 Alternative Energy Projects for Young Scientists*. Chicago: Chicago Review, 2010.

Internet Sources

Nova, "Power Surge," PBS, April 20, 2011. http://video.pbs.org/video/1873639434.

ProCon.org, "Alternative Energy: Pros and Cons," February 25, 2015. http://alternativeenergy.procon.org.

US Department of Energy, "Solar, Wind, Hydropower: Home Renewable Energy Installations," April 17, 2013. http://energy.gov/articles/solar-wind-hydropower-home-renewable-energy-installations.

Websites

American Council on Renewable Energy (www.acore.org). An American nonprofit organization providing excellent links to specific renewable energy projects around the United States as well as updated news on renewable energy projects.

International Energy Agency (www.iea.org). Based in Paris, France, the International Energy Agency attempts to coordinate responses to energy shortages and work toward clean energy. Links include information on renewable energy projects of member countries.

National Academy of Sciences (www.nasonline.org). A nonprofit based in Washington, DC, that provides nonpartisan scientific information on a range of scientific subjects, including detailed information on sustainable energy.

Renewable Energy World (www.renewableenergyworld.com /rea/magazine). A publication of the renewable industry sector that contains articles on new developments in renewable energy and overviews of different technologies that are on the market or in the research stage.

US Department of Energy (http://energy.gov). This government portal features links to emissions standards, explanations of US energy use by source of energy, and other energy-related information.

Index